"I was born and raised in the world's largest secular democracy—India. This democracy, while secular, was really based on India's primary religions. The church in India, though not directly involved in politics, voted and prayed for the pro-Christian party to win. It was not until I came to the USA in 1973 that I began to understand what Lee May unpacks in *My God, My Politics*. The book you now hold in your hands encourages you to allow your faith to inform your politics. Lee May takes a bibliocentric approach to guide our political thoughts and processes. A much-needed book that is sure to remove confusion and provide Kingdom order."

—*Dr. Samuel Chand, www.samchand.com*

"We are at a critical time in the history as a nation. Many would agree that the needs of our nation demand a government for and by the people. Lee May, who is both minister and politician, writes a must-read book that helps us understand how important it is for us not to shy away but to get involved. The genius of this book is that it teaches us how our faith can be the compulsion and the compass for our involvement."

—*Cynthia L. Hale, Senior Pastor, Ray of Hope Christian Church*

"Lee May gives greater clarity and understanding around the debate about separation of Church and State. He moves beyond religious talk and gets to the heartbeat of what should be at the center of our politics—which is our faith. This book is an intriguing, enlightening, and practical guide for those who wish to utilize their faith to shape their politics. Finally, an informative and compelling book that convinces you that your faith should always lead the way. A must-read for people of all faiths."

—*Bernice A. King, Founder and President, Be A King Enterprises, LLC*

Preface

As a minister and elected official, I have had the opportunity to engage these two aspects of my life in a manner that history and tradition say have nothing to do with the other. I have had the occasion to see both worlds up close and personal, and I see the natural nexus between the two. It is my belief that faith can and should connect with every aspect of our life.

Although this work is entitled *My God, My Politics*, this book has very little to do with my own personal thoughts and beliefs concerning faith and politics. It is not my intent to force my faith upon any individual or group. The point of this book is not to force anyone to believe as I believe. The intent of this work is to empower all readers to effectively engage their faith, as they see it, within the world of government and politics. Prayerfully, as you read this book you will have an opportunity to create a set of political views that will be well-informed by your most fundamental and core faith perspective.

Lee May
Lithonia, Georgia
Winter, 2011

in me that says that we are to respect all life (Exodus 20:13). These values are already reflected in our government through various laws and policies that say as much in legal terms. Throughout our discussion of faith and politics, it should be made crystal clear that the promotion of one's faith—Christianity, Judaism, Islam, and so on—through government or politics is intolerable. However, the promotion of one's values through one's beliefs is very much tolerable and, I believe, should be encouraged through our democratic form of government.

PROGRESSION OF POLICY

DEMOCRACY
(Chapter focus: Democracy)

◉

BELIEFS

Driven by:
Faith in God, Family Values, Understanding Scripture

◉

IDEOLOGY

◉

POLICY

◉

POLITICS

CHAPTER ONE

Democracy

But the thing displeased Samuel when they said, "Give us a king to judge us." So Samuel prayed to the Lord. And the Lord said to Samuel, "Heed the voice of the people in all that they say to you; for they have not rejected you, but they have rejected Me, that I should not reign over them."

—1 Samuel 8.6–7

Democracy, a government for the people by the people, is the self-determined form of government for these United States of America. The founders of this great nation decided to have this form of government, determining that its leaders would be selected through periodic elections and voted on by the people. It is this representative form of government that allows the people's voices to be heard in the direction and operation of our government. It is this form of government that allows people's core belief systems to be represented in the governing of this nation. Forgive me for this almost simplistic beginning, but it is essential in understanding how one's faith can and should work to inform one's politics.

People vote for candidates they believe will best represent their beliefs and their interests. These may not be mutually exclusive ideas. In every election, we are given choices: whether we will vote for the person that best represents our own core value and belief system, or whether will we simply vote for the person who we think can best lead our government. This may or may not be one and the same person. For example, someone who shares my basic moral and social values may not be the best equipped and qualified to represent me. Therefore, a dilemma might arise as to what preference I may have come Election Day.

However, in every election we are faced with the same challenge—how will we vote? Our democracy, as a representative form of government, should do just what it says. It should represent our beliefs, our interests, our aspirations, our values. It should represent who we are as people. It is for this reason that I believe our form of government allows, even promotes, the use of our faith value system (our belief system) to influence our politics. As a representative form of government, our government and its leaders ought to reflect who we are as people. It ought to reflect our hopes and dreams. It ought to reflect an institution that promotes life, liberty, and the pursuit of happiness. Our government ought to represent our most basic belief system.

Therefore, it is our democracy that gives us permission, as taxpaying citizens, to form a set of beliefs that can be translated into a political ideology. It is this ideology that ultimately bands people together into various groups called political parties. It is these beliefs that ultimately translate into a succinct set of policy positions. History has allowed us to communicate our beliefs through the democratic process, and it is the fruit of this activity that has proven the only real sustainable form of government for this nation.

The first example of a type of democracy in the Bible is the example of King Saul. Your first reaction to this example is likely...how can a kingdom with a king be likened to a democracy? The question can be answered by looking at the context of Saul being declared the first king of the United Kingdom of Israel. Saul became king after the people of Israel asked God for

When one listens first, there is a better opportunity for the individual to truly hear the perspective of the other party within the conversation. This is part of what a democracy encourages—real dialogue about what is best for the nation according to the people. The more our democracy embraces the will of the people and not special and corporate interest, the better positioned our nation will be for fulfilling its creed.

PROGRESSION OF POLICY

DEMOCRACY
(Chapter focus: Separation of Church and State)

◑

BELIEFS

Driven by:
Faith in God, Family Values, Understanding Scripture

◑

IDEOLOGY

◑

POLICY

◑

POLITICS

CHAPTER TWO

Separation of Church and State

And Jesus answered and said to them, "Render to Caesar the things that are Caesar's, and to God the things that are God's." And they marveled at Him.
—**Mark 12:17**

R est assured this book does not violate the time-tested virtue of "separation of church and state." This line of demarcation has been espoused since before the days of Thomas Jefferson. The phrase "separation of church and state" says that we live under a society that keeps government and church separate and free of influence from one another.

Jesus' comment in the previously quoted passage concerning taxation has been interpreted as Jesus espousing a real separation of church and state. Here, Jesus is being tested by the Pharisees and Herodians, who were determined to catch and twist Jesus's words in hopes that he would say something at odds with God or the government. This verse came in response to a question of whether it was lawful for Jews to pay taxes to Caesar. Jesus' response has been interpreted by many as a clear line of separation concerning God and the government or, in modern terms, the Church and the State.

However, Jesus was not speaking of separating the sacred from the secular in this scripture. I believe Jesus was making a point to both the Pharisees and the disciples alike. When Jesus said to give Caesar his due and God His due, he was saying to give Caesar that which he had created and likewise give God His due.

When Jesus spoke about the division of dues for Caesar and for God, He was probably thinking about David when he wrote in Psalm 24:1, "The earth *is* the Lord's, and all its fullness, the world and those who dwell therein." What Jesus was likely saying was that the entire earth and everything in it is God's, so give him what He is due. The concept of giving Caesar his due and giving God His due is a ridiculous proposition. To compare and contrast anything or anyone with God is an unwinnable task. Nothing can compare to God. If Jesus were to say give Caesar his due and also give Peter, James, John, or any other human their due, then this would be an understandable proposition. However, to say that Caesar owns anything in relationship to God is a losing proposition. God is clearly superior to Caesar, just like God is clearly superior to the government of the United States. However, there is still a level of respect that must be held in relationship to the government. Although, comparatively speaking, God is greater than the government; God still respects the institution of government. As such, Jesus observed the laws of the land, both religious and governmental, of His time.

Therefore, the comments made in relation to God and Caesar were not meant to say that we should completely negate God in the public square, nor was Jesus saying that we ought to allow the church or the people of God to take over the government. I believe Jesus simply meant that there was a clear distinction between God and Caesar. As a result of this distinction, we must give that which is appropriate for both. Thus, it is appropriate to give God the most basic of Godly creations—our hearts and minds. Likewise, we must give to Caesar that which is appropriate concerning the laws of the land and our own responsibility accordingly.

The reference to Caesar, in this manner, is likened to that of the State, and God, of course, is connected to the Church. Therefore, following the premise of Jesus, there is no comparison of God and the State. God is the creator of all things, and although mankind may have "created" a thing or built a thing, it does not mean that God had no hand or influence over it. From the very beginning of this nation's history there has always been a strong identification with the Christian faith. Many of the nation's founders were Christians. Many of its leaders at all levels were professed Christians, from U.S. Presidents to business leaders to civic leaders. We have self-identified this nation's historical connection to the Christian faith by various images and symbols, such as:

- Displays of Ten Commandments
- Religious references on documents ("In God We Trust" on the dollar bill; "Inalienable rights given by God")
- Reference to God in Pledge of Allegiance ("One nation under God")
- Inspirational messages before governmental meetings

"In God We Trust" is a symbol of the historical relationship this nation has had with the Judeo-Christian faith. It signifies, from the beginning, the belief in the divine by the founders of this nation. This belief by our founders has caused there to be an indelible relationship, for better or for worse, between faith and politics. This nation has, in many ways, codified its belief in God, not only through the passage of laws, but also through common acts practiced and symbols seen throughout society.

Returning to the reference of Caesar and God, let's turn to Deuteronomy 8:18: "But thou shalt remember the Lord thy God: for it is he that giveth thee power to get wealth, that he may establish his covenant which he swore unto thy fathers, as it is this day." This passage is dealing with a people who have been guided through tremendous times by the hand of the Lord, but had forgotten who it was that was guiding them through. So God was reminding them that it was He (God) that gave them the power to do all that they had accomplished. (Read the entire chapter – Deuteronomy 8.)

Likewise, although we may be smarter than ever before in history, and although we may have more scientific and technological advances than ever, we would be sorely mistaken if we were to believe that it was all of our own doing. It was the Lord that gave us the ability to create more wealth than ever in history. It was the Lord that allowed us to create more cures for sickness and disease than ever before. It was the Lord that allowed big metal-framed structures (airplanes) to soar through the sky. Our hands may have created it and our minds may have thought it, but we can never negate the fact that it is the Lord that created our hands and our minds. One can separate an institution (the Church) from the state, but there is no earthly way that one can separate God from anything on this earth, not even from the state. This is what I believe Jesus was saying in Matthew 22:21—that nothing can separate God from our lives. I think He was facetiously daring them to try to separate anything from God.

But let's make a clear distinction here: Jesus was not talking about the synagogue or the temple when he was talking about giving Caesar his due and giving God His due. God and the Church are not one in the same in this case. God is God, and the Church is a physical structure or an institution, depending on its definition. Jesus, in this case, was referring to God, not the Church or a church in particular. This is not a clear example of separating the Church and the State. It, however, clearly distinguishes God from the State, which may simply be semantics, but it is important to note that our belief in God cannot be limited or blocked by the State in any measure. God is too big and too powerful to be limited by a creation of humanity—the State.

Since the very beginning of this nation's history, there has been a healthy tension between religion and the government. The early settlers of this nation left the British Empire partly to insure that their freedom of religion was protected from the influence or pressure of the political systems of that time. Since the early settlers' desire was to leave the tyranny of the Church of England, there has been a desire in this nation to separate the influence of the church from the state and the influence of the state from the church.

According to Stephen Carter, a law professor at Yale University and the author of the book *God's Name in Vain: The Wrongs and Rights of Religion in Politics* (Basic Books, 2000):

> *The true origin of the metaphor (wall of separation) does not lie with Thomas Jefferson's coinage, which occurred over a decade after the First Amendment was adopted. Rather its origin is in Protestant theology. Indeed, (imbedded) in the Reformation was the idea that God had created not one but two forms of authority, the spiritual and the temporal, each with its own sphere of . . . power. The Reformers believed that God was sovereign over both and that both (the church and the state) were required to exercise power in accordance with God's law; nevertheless, their purposes were quite different, the one to prepare people's souls for salvation, the other to maintain order in the material world.*

This separation of the church and the state, however, has its first reference as a national doctrine by President Thomas Jefferson in 1802 when he wrote in response to a group located in Danbury, Connecticut called the Danbury Baptist Association. This group initially wrote Jefferson about the lack of controls in their state's law concerning religious liberty. In his response letter Jefferson wrote: Believing with you that religion is a matter which lives solely between Man and his God, that he owes account to none other for his faith or his worship, that the legitimate powers of government reach actions only and not opinions, I contemplate with sovereign reverence that act of the whole American people which declared that their legislature should "make no law respecting an establishment of religion, or prohibiting the free exercise thereof this building a wall of separation between Church and State."

Jefferson, in layman's terms, simply says that religion is something that should be between the individual and God. He was also saying that government shall not influence the church and the church shall not influence the government. This, in essence, deals with both actions of government and actions of the church. It's important to understand this point. We are speaking of actions, not beliefs or thoughts. The actions of one (the church or the government) shall not influence the other. This does not prevent either institution from having clear opinions regarding the other. However, the institutions themselves cannot do anything in an organized manner to unduly influence the other.

This nation has a very healthy and long-lasting relationship with the Judeo-Christian leanings of religion, since the days Europeans made the great journey to America to escape religious oppression. As a result, it was the early settlers' desire to establish freedom to practice one's faith without fear of persecution. This desire was ultimately codified in the very first amendment when it was written, "Congress shall make no law respecting an establishment of religion, or prohibiting the free exercise thereof . . . "

This amendment, along with the premise of Separation of Church and State, speaks only to laws respecting an establishment or creation of religion or the prohibition thereof. It speaks nothing about the beliefs or frames of thought behind the actual politics or practices. The Preamble, the introduction to the United States Constitution, lays out a brief statement about the purpose and principle behind the Constitution. It states: "We the People of the United States, in Order to form a more perfect Union, establish Justice, insure domestic Tranquility, provide for the common defense, promote the general Welfare, and secure the Blessings of Liberty to ourselves and our Posterity, do ordain and establish this Constitution for the United States of America."

Essentially, it states that the Constitution was meant to form a better United States. The theme behind this short statement is for the general and common good of this nation. The Bill of Rights, the final parting statements and amendments to the Constitution, gives certain rights that people are guaranteed to enjoy. The Bill of Rights lays out a number of basic protections. These protections lay out certain rights and/or prohibitions to name a few:

- ✪ It prohibits Congress from making any law respecting an establishment of religion.
- ✪ It guarantees freedom of speech.
- ✪ It forbids the infringement of the right to keep and bear arms by Congress or citizens in a federal territory.
- ✪ It guarantees due process of law and prohibits the federal government from depriving any person of life, liberty, or property, without due process of law.
- ✪ It guarantees a speedy public trial and prohibits double jeopardy.

The basic premise behind the Bill of Rights is that people's actions should not unduly affect the basic freedoms or livelihoods of others. The basic rights afforded through the U.S. Constitution and its Amendments allow citizens the ability to be free from the threat of undue influence of people's actions over their life. These rights have, at their core, the fundamental freedoms that innately lead to certain freedom of actions, which are spelled out in the Bill of Rights.

When asked the question, in the light of this "wall of separation," whether it's appropriate to think of government, policy, or politics in faith terms, my response is a resounding *yes!* What makes this nation great is the underpinnings of our basic rights as penned in the Declaration of Independence, which says, "All men are endowed by the Creator with certain inalienable rights that among these are life, liberty and the pursuit of happiness."

The protection of these basic rights is tantamount to the future of our great nation; it is essential for the backdrop of our democracy. Thus, above all else, the protection of our rights, and the prohibition of anything encroaching on these rights, is essential.

The Constitution of the United States is simply a set of rules for governing this great nation. The underpinnings of these rules rest upon one key principle: that our government gets its power from the people. This main principle protects people from infringement of their day-to-day lives by individuals, organizations, and even government. Thus, the Constitution is a document that is meant to enhance this nation as well as the individual lives of American citizens. The Constitution is concerned about the actions of government as well as the actions of citizens in relation to one another. However, it does not provide for prohibitions of ideas and thoughts. The entirety of the First Amendment to the United States Constitution reads: "Congress shall make no law respecting an establishment of religion, or prohibiting the free exercise thereof; or abridging the freedom of speech, or of the press; or the right of the people peaceably to assemble, and to petition the Government for a redress of grievances." This law deals with the actual promotion of one's religion within the framework of government. However, this does not hold true in the promotion of one's values within government. As stated in the Introduction, one's faith in God is what helps establish certain beliefs or values within a person. So, as a Christian, I have a certain value regarding human life, concerning the value of all people, concerning the value of helping those most in need. These are some of the values that help to drive my thoughts concerning government and politics.

Thomas Jefferson, in his letter to the Danbury Baptist Association concerning the First Amendment, speaks about "building a wall of separation between church and state." In his letter he deals with the first half of the First Amendment, which speaks about the relationship between church and government. However, the second half of the amendment deals with the matter of free speech, which states, "…or abridging the freedom of speech, or of the press; or the right of the people peaceably to assemble, and to petition the Government for a redress of grievances."

Again, this amendment doesn't speak to actions of individuals or groups. This amendment deals with speech, not actions. It's just as important to focus on what it says as what it doesn't say. This amendment gives citizens the unabridged freedom to speak their thoughts on any subject matter. It doesn't, however, give the same freedom of actions. The Congress makes laws every year constricting various actions by its citizenry. The right of Congress to prohibit certain actions says that people are not free to do anything they desire. People are limited in their actions based upon how it affects, impedes, or encroaches on another individual or group. However, this amendment makes it clear that people have the right to speak or assemble freely without the risk of censorship or any type of punishment. As simplistic as this may sound, speech is connected to thought. Even when someone speaks out of turn or speaks before thinking, there was some thought that was connected to it. If one has the right of free speech, then they also have the right of free thought. Thus, if free speech is a fundamental right, then free thought must be as well. Speech is a direct by-product of thought. The First Amendment doesn't make some speech better or worse than other speech. As unpopular as it may be, people may even have the freedom of speech to spew hate, within reasonable limits. Freedom of speech is connected to freedom of thought. Therefore, if there is a fundamental right to speak, there is also a fundamental right to think. To take stances based upon personal ideological viewpoints—i.e. one's faith perspective—is perfectly fine to do and furthermore is supported by the U.S. Constitution itself.

Therefore, by allowing your faith to inform your politics you are not only in lockstep with the mindset of the nation's founders, you are in harmony with the Constitution itself. There is no violation of the First Amendment, or of the separation of church and state doctrine, when one's faith is allowed to influence one's politics. The violation only occurs when one's actions or policies violate the fundamental rights afforded within the Constitution itself. When we allow our faith to influence our politics, we are actually operating within the fundamental principles of our Constitution which grants religious liberty as well as freedom of speech.

Dr. D. James Kennedy, pastor of Coral Ridge Ministries, stated in his sermon entitled "Bible and Politics," "Every law ever enacted imposes somebody's morality on somebody else; legislation is built upon morality and morality is built upon religion. There is no escape from that fact." Dr. Kennedy is speaking from a standpoint that for every law that is enacted there is a certain morality that is also imposed on society. He gives the example of a law that prohibits prostitution. He says that a law prohibiting prostitution imposes a morality of a higher standard concerning sex. Therefore, this law essentially imposes a morality concerning sex on persons who don't necessarily have a high standard of sex. A law against murder imposes a higher moral view of life on those persons who have a lower view or standard regarding life.

Our laws, as rules of conduct, focus entirely on actions of individuals, not on beliefs or thoughts. Thus, the First Amendment specifically protects the rights of speech. It implicitly protects the right of people to believe. Ironically, the same Amendment used to promote the separation of church and state doctrine can also be used to promote the right to use one's faith to inform one's political and public policy positions. Furthermore, not only does the First Amendment protect religious liberties and freedom of speech, it also empowers Americans to use their core values and their faith to influence their policies and politics.

Quotations from Political Leaders of the Past:

It is impossible to rightly govern the world without God and the Bible.

—George Washington (1732–1799), First U.S. President

I have always said and always will say that the studious perusal of the Sacred Volume will make better citizens, better fathers, better husbands . . . the Bible makes the best people in the world.

—Thomas Jefferson (1743–1826), Third U.S. President

So great is my veneration of the Bible that the earlier my children begin to read it the more confident will be my hope that they will prove useful citizens of their country.

—John Quincy Adams (1767–1848), Sixth U.S. President

The Bible is the rock on which our republic rests.

—Andrew Jackson (1767–1845), Seventh U.S. President

I believe the Bible is the best book God has ever given to man. All the good from the Savior of the world is communicated to us through this book.

—Abraham Lincoln (1809–1865), Sixteenth U.S. President

Our ancestors established their system of government on morality and religious sentiment. Moral habits, they believed, cannot safely be trusted on any other foundation than religious principle, not any government secure which is not supported by moral habits . . . Whatever makes men good Christians, makes them good citizens.

—Daniel Webster (1782–1852), American statesman and political leader

PROGRESSION OF POLICY

DEMOCRACY

◖

BELIEFS
(Chapter focus: My God)

Driven by:
Faith in God, Family Values, Understanding Scripture

◖

IDEOLOGY

◖

POLICY

◖

POLITICS

CHAPTER THREE

My God

"Teacher, which is the greatest commandment in the Law?" Jesus replied: "Love the Lord your God with all your heart and with all your soul and with all your mind. This is the first and greatest commandment. And the second is like it: Love your neighbor as yourself. All the Law and the Prophets hang on these two commandments."

—Matthew 22:36–40

The story of the Christian faith begins with God in what we know as the creation story. In this story, God shows his all-powerful hand in creating the universe from the earth itself, to the seas, to vegetation, to animals, to humanity. In this creation story, God shows His love for His creation by making the recurring statement, "It was good." After each creation action, God seems to take a step back, in anthropomorphic terms, and say, "It was good." This shows that everything that was made by the "hand" of God can be accepted as good. If God made it, then we know that, as stewards over God's creation, we ought to respect and honor it as being "good."

In the early stages of creation, God established some preliminary boundaries for Adam and Eve, which served as basic standards for life as they knew it. God told them to "tend and keep" the garden (Genesis 2:15). He also told them that they could eat of any tree in the garden except for the "tree of the knowledge of good and evil" (Genesis 2:16). As we know, Adam and Eve disobeyed this directive and were cast out of the garden. However, God did not simply cast the two away. God remained in a relationship with them, although it was very unlike the relationship they had in the Garden of Eden.

The story of Adam, Eve, Cain, Abel, Noah, Abraham, Isaac, Jacob, Joseph, Moses, and everyone between and after is a story of sin and death, redemption and life. It is one where humanity has disappointed and failed God, and God still has forgiven and restored humanity. It is a story of people who loved God and embraced their Creator, but it's also a story of those who hated and denied their Creator. It is a story of God's love for His people and for His creation. It is a love story, where God desires to see the best in all of His creation.

God is an all-powerful, all-knowing, omnipresent (present everywhere), omniscient (all-knowing), and omnipotent (all-powerful) being. There is nothing that can compare to the magnitude or the presence of God. Although this may sound a bit preachy, it is the fundamental truth. This understanding of God does not happen simply through the reading of the Bible, although it is informative. This truth can only be accepted as true through a true and authentic relationship with him. God has proven his love toward humanity time and time again through countless encounters that are told and retold in Scripture, from the Great Flood and Noah to the coming of Jesus Christ for the salvation of all of humanity.

Personally, my God gives direction to my life. My relationship with God and my understanding of what God holds to be true serves as a guide for my life. I wrote about the fundamentals of the faith to share the basics of my faith, to enlighten you on what the foundational elements are within the Christian faith. There is no faith without that which was in the beginning . . . God! Furthermore, the Christian faith is the only faith with the advent of Jesus Christ . . . the Son of God! By understanding some of the basic fundamentals of the faith, it becomes a little easier to understand why Christians believe as they do concerning the nature of humanity, the nature of relationships, the nature of the environment, the nature of the world, and more.

My God is the moral and spiritual compass for my life. My compass is informed, in large part, by my relationship with God. This may be somewhat difficult to grasp, especially for those persons who deal heavily in logic and reason. For many, even Christians, it is difficult to grasp the concept of having a relationship with God. However, I will submit that your relationship with God can be and should be a very real thing. It is not out of the realm of imagination to think that a person can have a very vibrant relationship with God. Of course, this relationship looks quite different from a typical relationship that humans will have with one another. However, a relationship with God is a very practical thing to have.

Building a relationship with God is a difficult process to describe. In the simplest of terms, it is doing what it takes to grow closer to God. It is committing one's entire life to God. You might ask, how can this be done? You can do this by focusing all of your attention and energy to God through prayer, meditation, and reading of the Holy Word. It comes by doing what God commanded us to do in His word—primarily to love God and to love thy neighbor. If we do what God asked us to do in His Word, we will grow closer to God, and I truly believe we will begin to think and act in a manner that would absolutely thrill God.

As a side note, much of what I know about God is informed by the Word of God, also known as the Bible or the Scriptures. My relationship with God is strengthened based upon my reading, interpreting, and meditating on the Word of God.

My God Explained

As I will continue to repeat throughout this book, my belief in God has a great influence over every aspect of my life. My view on God's place and power in the world is fundamental to my understanding of how the world ought to operate. My understanding concerning God's power can be described through the Scriptures that follow.

I am the Alpha and the Omega, the Beginning and the End, the First and the Last.

—*Revelation 22:13*

The earth is the Lord's, and all its fullness, the world and those who dwell therein.

—*Psalm 24:1*

Indeed heaven and the highest heavens belong to the Lord your God, also the earth with all that is in it.

—*Deuteronomy 10:14*

Who has preceded Me, that I should pay him? Everything under heaven is Mine.

—*Job 41:11*

God is all-powerful, all-knowing. There was nothing that preceded God. God is the creator of all things. God created the heavens and the earth and everything that is on the earth. Thus, my God and my politics can never be mutually exclusive. My God and my politics are inextricably connected. God, through the work of His creation, is the creator of politics. The way that I see it, there is nothing that exists that is not connected to God. One can simply look at the creation account in the book of Genesis. The creation account, again, starts by saying, "In the beginning God created the heavens and the earth." This account lets us know that there was nothing in existence before God began His creation activity. If God is the creator of all things on earth, it is not out of the question to think that He ought to have some level of influence over it.

Every person of faith ought to have God as their foundation in the performance of their respective jobs and responsibilities. I am no different in my personal life, whether as a man in the ministry, as a small business owner, or as an elected official. The primary resource in my life for making decisions of all types and sizes is my relationship with God. It is my faith that leads me.

The reason I decided to run for office was because of my belief that God had something for me to offer my country. I believe that everything God created me to be is sufficient to serve the people of my county, my state, and my country. God has called me to operate in this role, in this moment in history. My faith is the core of my entire being, and it is always my desire to make decisions in life through the lens of my faith. Four Scriptures in particular highlight the reason why I made the leap into public service through the means of elected office:

Open your mouth for the speechless, in the cause of all appointed to die. Open your mouth, judge righteously, and plead the cause for the poor and needy.

—Proverbs 31:8–9

The Spirit of the Lord is upon Me because He has anointed Me to preach the gospel to the poor; He has sent me to heal the broken-hearted, to proclaim liberty to the captives and recovery of sight to the blind, to set at liberty those who are oppressed; to proclaim the acceptable year of the Lord.

—Luke 4:18–19

He has shown you, O man, what is good; and what does the Lord require of you but to do justly, love mercy and to walk humbly with your God?

—Micah 6:8

Trust in the Lord with all your heart, and lean not on your own understanding. In all your ways acknowledge Him, and He shall direct your paths. Do not be wise in your own eyes; fear the Lord and depart from evil.

—*Proverbs 3:5–7*

The first two Scriptures lay out essentially what I have been called to do in the political arena. I am called to speak for those who don't have the capacity to speak for themselves. I am called to help those who have been considered the "least of these" (i.e. the poor, the brokenhearted, the captive, the blind, and the oppressed). I am called to help those most vulnerable, those most in need. These Scriptures served as the foundation for my initial campaign for office and also the mission of my current practice while in office. The third and fourth Scripture references remind me that the Lord simply requires me to do justly and to stay connected to Him (God) in all that I say and do. It is through this posture of seeking God that He will direct my path.

My politics follow my faith. My faith tells me to focus on the "least of these" and to walk closely with Him (God). This leads me to ask two questions each and every time I must make a binding decision in my role as an elected official. The first question asks: How will this decision affect the "least of these"? The second question asks: Will God be pleased with my decision?

PROGRESSION OF POLICY

DEMOCRACY

↓

BELIEFS
(Chapter focus: My Life)

Driven by:
Faith in God, Family Values, Understanding Scripture

↓

IDEOLOGY

↓

POLICY

↓

POLITICS

CHAPTER FOUR

My Life

For I know the thoughts that I think toward you, says the Lord, thoughts of peace and not of evil, to give you a future and a hope.

—*Jeremiah 29:11*

The above passage is one given by God to the prophet Jeremiah for the people of Israel. God's message to the children of Israel was that, despite their predicament and situation at the time, God still had a plan for their lives. The people of Israel during this period were in a state of exile. They had been taken away from their native land to a foreign land. Jeremiah's message to them was one of hope despite their situation. God, through Jeremiah, told them that despite their current state of exile He still had a plan for their lives. This reminds me of the tripartite motto, "Life, Liberty, and the Pursuit of Happiness," proclaimed in the Declaration of Independence as part of our unalienable rights. God is saying to Israel that regardless of what their situation appeared to be, He was still on their side. It says that despite your current plight, despite the mistakes you may have made . . . God has a plan for you. God says, in the passage, that he has plans of a future and of hope for His people, the people of Israel; or, in the words of the Declaration of Independence, a plan for life, liberty, and the pursuit of happiness.

This Scripture can be connected to an earlier period, when Joshua was taking over the leadership from Moses pending his death. In Deuteronomy 31:6, Moses says to the people of Israel, "Be strong and of good courage, do not fear nor be afraid of them; for the Lord your God, He *is* the One who goes with you. He will not leave you nor forsake you." This passage says to the hearers and readers of this verse, that God will always be with His people, whether in good or bad times. I believe that God has a plan for each and every one of our lives—a plan that may not be recognizable at times, nor even pleasant, but a plan, nonetheless, that is for our benefit if we so choose to act accordingly.

My Early Life

I am the son of a pastor (Rev. Lee May, Sr.) and an educator (Dianne May). I am the brother of a U.S. Navy veteran (Keith) and a U.S. Army veteran (Jamarra, a.k.a. Jay). I am the brother of an educator (LaKecia) and the husband of a professional counselor (Robin). Service to others is in the DNA of the May family gene pool. Service, as a vocation, was not something that was actually discussed within our family. It was simply understood that the path to living a fulfilling life was located on the road to serving others. Our vocational paths were chosen not through open dialogue, but through simple observation and agreement. We simply chose life plans that followed the paths of our parents and of many of our extended family.

My father has been a pastor in the AME (African Methodist Episcopal) Church for over thirty years. As pastor, I saw my father work diligently to meet the needs of his congregation, on both a spiritual and a very practical level, in a manner that addressed their daily needs. I would see my father get up in the late hours of the night to visit a parishioner in need. I would see him give money out of his own pocket to members that were in need of financial assistance at the time. I would see him give wise counsel to married couples within the congregation who needed help mending their broken marriage. I would see him spend time with children within the church who he knew were from single-family homes and needed extra attention. I saw my father's entire life dedicated to people, dedicated to the betterment of other people's lives, dedicated to service to others, dedicated to creating the "beloved community" that Dr. Martin Luther King hoped to create through his work.

I never understood, as a child, why I was made to move from city to city, state to state, school to school, church to church. Seven cities, five states, nine schools, and six churches describe the journey of my life. The word "transition" could sum up the early years of my life. It was my father's vocation as a pastor in the AME Church that caused the constant movement in our lives. The AME Church functions under the itinerant system, which means traveling from place to place to cover a circuit. Essentially, my father and other pastors within the denomination were subject to being moved within their respective districts, covering a specific geographical area around the nation.

Our family's life followed the wind of my father's ministerial career. As my father was moved from church to church, our entire lives were uprooted to be replanted, many times hundreds of miles away from our previous home. A move to a new city meant a new teaching position for my mother, new schools for my siblings and me, new homes, new neighborhoods, and new friends for the entire family. Although my father was committed to his calling to the ministry of the Gospel, this was a commitment that was made by the entire family. We were all a part of the ministry. We were all deeply invested in living out the calling of my father's vocational pursuits.

I never understood why my father never complained or grumbled when he was asked to move from one church to another, typically outside of the city in which we lived. However, as I matured as a man, I understood why my father simply smiled and said, "Yes, I will go." My father operated as a minister under the premise that his entire life was directed by his faith and his calling. This perspective on life was not only that of my father's, but that of our entire household.

When my father was asked to move, my mother also smiled and said, "Okay, let's go." My mother believed in living life according to what she believed was the will of God for her life. My mother has been an educator for over thirty years. My mother began her career in education at the same time my father began his career in ministry. She spent the lion's share of her educational career in the classroom specializing in behavioral and learning disabilities in students with special needs. These are the children most in need of love and support to assist them in their learning challenges. Unfortunately, as we all know, teaching is a thankless job, one that's overworked and underpaid. My mother dedicated her life for over thirty years to service to others by educating the youth of this nation. My mother has stated that being an educator is a calling of God. Therefore, when my father was asked to change churches, it did not cause my mother to panic. She didn't feel that our constant relocations ever altered the call of God over her life to teach. She simply felt that, regardless of what city or school she was a part of, all of God's children needed to be educated.

The offspring of Dianne and Lee Sr. have also followed in their own personal forms of service to others. Lee II, LaKecia, Keith, and Jamarra have all chosen service-oriented vocational paths in life. As Preacher's Kids (PKs), we obviously were raised in the church. As a matter of fact, we were actively engaged in the life of the church. From the youth usher board to the youth department to the youth choir; we were active in a plethora of ministries within the church. Our upbringing in the church exposed us to the basic tenets of God and the Holy Scriptures. It introduced us to the stories, characters, and wisdom of Scripture. It exposed us to concepts such as salvation, faith, grace, and many other beliefs related to the Christian story.

The older I grew, the more understanding I gained from my ecclesiastical experience. As I attended Sunday Schools and Vacation Bible Schools, listened to innumerable amount of sermons, and read the Bible countless times, I gradually became more and more versed in Scripture and matters of faith. As my life evolved from adolescence to adulthood and from under the care of my parents to a life of independence, my life began to reflect more of the values that were espoused and taught within my church experience. As my relationship within the Christian experience grew, my behavior and actions also grew accordingly. I began to act more like what the Scriptures espoused. My parents used Scripture as a guide for their lives. Their faith was their guide and the influence of Scripture was a critical component of their lives. This is what led them to pursue their career paths. My family's faith perspective rubbed off on me and influenced my understanding concerning life.

It was the faith of my parents that prompted them to undertake a life of service to others. Their faith was the catalyst for their call to service. Their service came as a result of their faith. Their faith was matured through their reading, interpreting, and understanding of Scripture. Their service came as a result of the indelible impression that their Christian faith made upon their lives. They literally took their faith and made it come alive within their day-to-day lives. They made their faith alive in their marriage, in their relationship with their children, in their relationships with friends, and in their careers. They effectively translated their faith from a simple theoretical construct into real praxis. They took a pie-in-the-sky concept and made it a reality in their own lives. My siblings and I learned from the lives of our parents. Although we didn't quite understand why they did many of the things they did in their lives, we clearly understood it was something they felt a special calling to do.

It was this same understanding that caused my sister to enter the world of education. My sister followed my steps at Clark Atlanta University (the best university in the world) and also majored in Business Administration with a concentration in Finance. Upon graduation, she accepted a job on Wall Street with the New York Stock Exchange. She progressed within her career, and in the first three years she literally doubled her income. She was moving forward in her career with exceptional speed when she made the decision to alter her career path. She decided that she wanted to pursue a career in education. She wanted to leave the world of self-concern, self-gratification, and self-indulgence. She traded that world for a world of sacrifice and service for others. She decided she wanted to work to make the lives of our youth better. She made the decision that inevitably followed the same path as our mother.

My parents have always operated under the auspices of "Love thy God" and "Love thy Neighbor." My parents, although not perfect, understood that it is better to give than to receive. They understood the Biblical principle: "Give and it shall be given unto you, good measure, pressed down and shaken together" (Luke 6:38).

Preparation for Politics

Upon graduating from high school in Kansas City, Kansas, I was awarded a full academic scholarship to Clark Atlanta University (CAU) in Atlanta, Georgia. It was here that I majored in Business Administration with a Marketing concentration. I chose my major based upon a couple of factors. First, I have always had a love for business. At my high school, Sumner Academy of Arts and Science, I owned my own candy business. I was somewhat of a traveling candy sales representative. That's a complicated way of saying that I sold Blow Pops and penny candy from a pouch I carried faithfully from class to class while I was in school. It was a very lucrative venture. I would purchase a box of Blow Pops (100-

count) for six dollars from Sam's Club. I would sell each Blow Pop for a quarter. You can do the math—each box would yield a nineteen-dollar profit. All I would have to do is simply go to class and make my product available for purchase. I would sell a box a day. That was my foray into business.

The second reason for the selection of business as my major was because of my father. As a preacher's kid, I was inundated with the question, "Are you going to be a preacher like your daddy?" My response was always a resounding "*NO.*" As a child and teenager, I had no desire to follow my father's footsteps. I didn't like that he was a pastor because of the attention it brought to my family and me. That's very ironic considering the ultimate path I have chosen for my life. As a result, when it was time to select a major, I figured I would choose the field that was the most diametrically opposed to my father's vocation. Thus, I chose business as my field of study. Upon completing my study at CAU in 1998, I worked in corporate America for a couple of years. Then I did the unthinkable: I decided to return to school to get my masters of divinity degree from the Candler School of Theology at Emory University. This is the academic degree that people typically receive in preparation for their ministry. Yes, I said ministry! Somehow, between my younger days and my college years, I began to feel a change in direction for my life. My desire for a vocational path didn't change, it was altered. It had now expanded from my previous singular path of business to a dual vocational path of business and ministry. While working on my masters degree, I was subsequently licensed as a minister within my local church of 25,000 people. I completed my academic work and graduated with honors in May, 2003. Consequently, in a surprise move by my pastor, I was ordained an Elder at my church, making me the youngest Elder in our congregation. Ironically, my church, which was very active in the community, also happened to be located in the heart of the district that I would eventually run for office as commissioner.

Whether it was my original intent or not, I ultimately followed the path of my father. I didn't just copy the path of my father. The direction of my journey really was set, in part by the example of my father and mother. For my vocation, it simply manifested in the form of business and ministry. After the completion of my masters of divinity degree, I immediately began working as a community organizer for an organization that sought to increase access to health care for the 40+ million Americans who lacked health insurance. The campaign was called Georgians for Health Care (GHC). This campaign was an initiative of the Service Employees International Union (SEIU). This was my first foray into the world of the organized labor movement and politics. SEIU is a labor union that focuses heavily on health care as one of its major policy initiatives. As a part of this campaign, we registered over 50,000 people to vote across the entire state of Georgia, and we educated them on health care as a real election and public policy issue and the need for real reform.

I worked on the GHC campaign for two years, primarily organizing people within the black church. I did this for two years before I began taking steps to realize one of my major life goals, which was to own my own business. In 2005, I opened my first business. I acquired an eight-screen movie theater in Lithonia, Georgia, which also was, located in the heart of what would be my future commission district. When I opened the theater it was quite a feat for two reasons. First, at twenty-nine years of age, I was the youngest movie theater owner in the nation. Second, I was only one of three African-American movie theater owners in the nation. Magic Johnson is one of the three African American movie theater owners in the nation. Magic was actually part of the inspiration for me pursuing this great endeavor. This venture ultimately served as preparation for my eventual run for county commissioner.

While I was still a young, aspiring-to-be-successful business owner, I received a call from a close friend of mine, Erik Burton.

His voice was bubbling with excitement. He told me that the person who was my representative on the county board of commissioners, Henry "Hank" Johnson, announced that he would be running for Congress. Since the election for this new office was in the middle of his term, he had to resign from his county commission seat. Thus, the excitement behind Erik's voice was one of opportunity. "You ought to run for his seat!" he said. He told me of the void that would be left on the commission. In earnest, I had an interest in running for public office in the past but had not given real thought at that time; I was simply focused on growing my business. At the time I hadn't given much thought to local politics either. I was focused solely on state and national politics, while mostly ignoring the realities and responsibilities of the locally elected official and government. Immediately after my conversation with Erik, I went to the county's website to find out just what a county commissioner did.

I quickly found that local politics was a tremendous way to make a real difference in the day-to-day lives of people. I began to get excited at the possibility of serving on a local basis in the political arena. Up to that point I had only helped people engage public policy as an organizer in the community. While in that role I built coalitions with people and groups that were advocates for affordable access to health care. I gained experience in political campaigns during this period by helping others realize their political ambitions. I worked as the field director for U.S. Congresswoman Denise Majette in her campaign for the U.S. Senate. Although we all knew this endeavor would be a long shot, it was my goal to help her run an efficient and respectable campaign. I took over this role between the primary election and the general election in 2004 as a result of some internal changes in her campaign.

My world was unknowingly being prepared for the world of public office. As a business owner I had to promote my business, and as a candidate for office I would have to promote myself. As a business owner I had to learn how to offer excellent customer service; as a candidate and elected official I had to deal with constituents and their basic needs and concerns as taxpaying citizens. As a community organizer I learned how to build coalitions and get people interested and involved in issues that directly affected their lives.

My Goal

My goal is to make my God relevant in every aspect of my life. It is my faith that has steered the ship of just about every aspect of my life. It is my faith that has served to guide my life's decisions. Specifically in my adult years, I have desired to make both major and minor decisions according to what I believe to be the will of God for my life. My college major, my career choices—even my soul mate, my beautiful wife, were all chosen through the foundation of my faith.

When I made the decision to ask my wife, Robin Simpson, to marry me, she was absolutely beautiful, with the most engaging and loving personality of any woman I've known. However, that would have been for naught had I not felt that she was a woman that God would be pleased for me to marry. In the end, the final decision to marry was made in the quiet hours of prayer and meditation. When I made the decision to leave my corporate job in sales to pursue a masters of divinity degree, it was what I believed God wanted me to do in preparation of my call to the ministry. When I decided to enter the world of entrepreneurship, while it was part personal ambition, it was also God-inspired; when I decided to run for elected office as a county commissioner in DeKalb County, Georgia, it was because I believed that this was what God desired for me to do at that time of my life. Thus, my life has been directed and influenced by my relationship, my faith, and my commitment to God. My belief and faith in the Almighty has given me the capacity to make decisions and commitments in life that I believe are right in the eyes of God.

But seek first the kingdom of God and His righteousness, and all these things shall be added to you.

—*Matthew 6:33*

Trust in the Lord with all your heart, and lean not on your own understanding; in all your ways acknowledge Him, and He shall direct your paths.

—*Proverbs 3:5–6*

These verses have always let me know the importance of seeking God concerning every area of my life. They let me know that in every area of my life, I am capable of searching the will of God for my life and he subsequently will lead me in the direction I ought to take. These verses are imperative sentences. This means they are expressing a request or a command. They give an imperative to "Seek first the Kingdom of God" and to "Trust in the Lord with all your heart." However, they also give the result of seeking and trusting the Lord, which is that many things will be "added to you" and that God will "direct your paths." When the Lord is adding to and directing your life, you can be assured of sure success.

These verses say to me that, as a Christian, I can seek the Lord's counsel and expect that the end result is one that is in my best interest. They say to me that my path will be fruitful, productive, and prosperous when I seek the Lord. They also tell me that the end results of my choices and decisions, whether pertaining to me or to others, will be pleasing in God's eyes. The question then becomes—in what area of life should I seek the Lord's wisdom? Should my search for the Lord concerning various subject matters be confined to only certain safe subjects?

What I have learned in my life is that God shouldn't be confined simply to those areas concerning the church or even to the personal piety of the individual. Genesis 1:1 says, "In the beginning God created the heavens and the earth." Genesis 2:2

reads, "And on the seventh day God ended His work which He had done, and He rested on the seventh day from all His work which He had done." Thus, God created the heavens, the earth, and everything that was made. I interpret this Scripture to mean that everything that was and is still to be created was done so either directly by God (in the original creation story) or indirectly by the creativity of humankind or nature.

I am called to be a good steward over all God has given me and placed in my position of authority. As a man of God and as a servant of the people, I must give a full account for all that I have done regarding my life and concerning the lives of people for whom I am responsible. It is a much easier task to make a decision when it only affects my life. The dilemma in this faith talk is when my decisions, having been rooted in faith, affect not only my life but other people's lives, communities, and institutions. Therefore, I have to be confident that although all may not share my faith perspective, the decisions I make based on faith are fair and just toward all people, even those who do not believe as I believe.

My life can be described as a three-legged stool, which is built on the legs of business, ministry, and politics. From a cursory perspective, one may ask what these three areas have to do with one another. My response is simple—my life is built on service to others. In each of these areas there lies some degree of service to others. When I acquired my movie theater, my mindset for prospering was not just for personal gain; it was so that I could create a quality business venture in my community. I desired to have a quality movie theater in our neighborhood that the community could be proud of supporting. It was also my desire to create jobs for the local residents and youth, by which I could also mentor many of my young workers. It was my desire to have a business that supported the community through our philanthropic efforts.

In ministry, it is simply my desire to minister to God's people through their mental, physical, and spiritual needs. My desire has always been to accomplish this both within the confines of the church and outside of the church.

In politics, I simply want to lead the people in a manner that pleases God and builds a better America. Micah 6:8 and Proverbs 31:8–9 adequately sum up my thoughts and plans concerning my role in politics through elected office.

He has shown you, O man, what is good; and what does the Lord require of you? But to do justly, to love mercy, and to walk humbly with your God.

—Micah 6:8

Open your mouth for the speechless, in the cause of all who are appointed to die. Open your mouth, judge righteously, and plead the cause of the poor and needy.

—Proverbs 31:8–9

My desire is to do justly toward all people I represent and to walk with God in a manner that pleases him. And it is my desire to speak in my seat of power on the behalf of those who cannot speak for themselves.

PROGRESSION OF POLICY

DEMOCRACY

⊍

BELIEFS
(Chapter Focus: Scripture 101)

Driven by:
Faith in God, Family Values, Understanding Scripture

⊍

IDEOLOGY

⊍

POLICY

⊍

POLITICS

CHAPTER FIVE

Scripture 101 (Understanding Scripture)

All Scripture is given by inspiration of God, and is profitable for doctrine, for reproof, for correction, for instruction in righteousness, that the man of God may be complete, thoroughly equipped for every good work.

—2 Timothy 3:16–17

The Bible is the single most influential book in the history of western thought. Its ideas, themes, and principles shape the way most of the world thinks about itself, its communities, and its people. In addition to teaching how God has saved His people from their sins and the consequences thereof, the Bible also teaches how to live as peaceful, civilized human beings on Earth. The laws that God gave to Moses, the Ten Commandments, serve as an indispensable basis for a civilized society.

The principles of faith are grounded in the stories, characters, and wisdom of the Holy Bible. However, many have a difficult time connecting faith with day-to-day living. The Bible, again, says, "All Scripture is inspired by God and is profitable." This means that all Scripture has the capacity to speak relevantly to our lives. However, because of the abuse and misuse by certain men and women of faith over the years, the world to a large degree has become skeptical concerning faith. The world is now hesitant to allow faith to be injected into the dialogue of the world. This has caused many to develop a mental roadblock when faith is brought into the public square for discourse, especially concerning life's daily issues. Scripture itself is not the barrier to wisdom for our lives. It is man's poor interpretation of Scripture that has caused a divide as wide as the Atlantic Ocean. This divide is to our detriment. The Bible is filled with anecdotes, stories, wisdom, and teachings that truly add value to our lives. It enriches our family situations, builds better communities, and helps us to form a "more perfect union."

Throughout the sixty-six books of the Bible, from Genesis to Revelation, there are major learning opportunities for life. They offer us a better understanding of God's nature, of humanity, and of the world. However, in order to truly have a faith-informed life, we must adequately know, understand, and be able to apply the Bible to our personal lives. We must understand its daily applications to our lives. Before we can begin to engage Scripture in an effort to inform our lives, we must understand the basic tenets of the faith as espoused in Scripture.

The Bible is not simply a regular book in the sense that a man or woman wrote it from his or her own mind or imagination. It is the spirit inspired Word of God.

For prophecy never came by the will of man, but holy men of God spoke as they were moved by the Holy Spirit.

—2 Peter 1:21

Once we have a good understanding of the origins of the Bible, we must have a basic knowledge about what is contained in it. The Bible, as previously mentioned, begins with the words, "In the beginning God created the heavens and the earth." Two things are immediately established in this text. First, it establishes that there is a higher being. Second, it establishes that this higher being is the creator of the heavens and the earth. These are two fundamental premises to the Christian faith—and to most religions, for that matter. Isaiah 44:24 reconfirms this description of God when it says, "Thus says the Lord, your Redeemer, and He who formed you from the womb: I am the Lord, who makes all things, who stretches out the heavens all alone, who spreads abroad the earth by Myself."

The following scriptures are highlighted to give some of the basic tenets of the faith. These scriptures are the foundation of what I and many Christians believe concerning God.

There is only one God:

"You are My witnesses," says the Lord, "And My servant whom I have chosen, that you may know and believe Me, and understand that I am He. Before Me there was no God formed, nor shall there be after Me."

—*Isaiah 43:10*

Thus says the Lord, the King of Israel, and his Redeemer, the Lord of hosts: "I am the First and I am the Last; Besides Me there is no God."

—*Isaiah 44:6*

God is omniscient, which means "knows all things":

Known to God from eternity are all His works.

—*Acts 15:18*

He counts the number of the stars; He calls them all by name. Great is our Lord, and mighty in power; His understanding is infinite.

—*Psalm 147:4–5*

You know my sitting down and my rising up; You understand my thought afar off. You comprehend my path and my lying down, and are acquainted with all my ways. For there is not a word on my tongue, but behold, O Lord, You know it altogether.

—*Psalm 139:2–4*

God is omnipotent, which means "all-powerful":

Behold, I am the Lord, the God of all flesh. Is there anything too hard for Me?

—*Jeremiah 32:27*

But our God is in heaven; He does whatever He pleases.

—*Psalm 115:3*

And I heard, as it were, the voice of a great multitude, as the sound of many waters and as the sound of mighty thunderings, saying, "Alleluia! For the Lord God Omnipotent reigns!"

—*Revelation 19:6*

God is omnipresent, which means "present everywhere":

Where can I go from Your Spirit? Or where can I flee from Your presence? If I ascend into heaven, You are there; If I make my bed in hell, behold, You are there.

— *Psalm 139.7–8*

God is sovereign:

I urge you in the sight of God who gives life to all things, and before Christ Jesus who witnessed the good confession before Pontius Pilate, that you keep this commandment without spot, blameless until our Lord Jesus Christ's appearing, which He will manifest in His own time, He who is the blessed and only Potentate, the King of kings and Lord of lords, who alone has immortality, dwelling in unapproachable light, whom no man has seen or can see, to whom be honor and everlasting power. Amen.

—*1 Timothy 6:13–16*

Thus I prostrated myself before the Lord; forty days and forty nights I kept prostrating myself, because the Lord had said He would destroy you. Therefore I prayed to the Lord, and said: "O Lord God, do not destroy Your people and Your inheritance whom You have redeemed through Your greatness, whom You have brought out of Egypt with a mighty hand."

—*Deuteronomy 9:25–26*

God is immutable, which means "unchangeable":

Every good gift and every perfect gift is from above, and comes down from the Father of lights, with whom there is no variation or shadow of turning.

— *James 1:17*

For I am the Lord, I do not change; therefore you are not consumed, O sons of Jacob.

—*Malachi 3:6*

Thus God, determining to show more abundantly to the heirs of promise the immutability of His counsel, confirmed it by an oath, that by two immutable things, in which it is impossible for God to lie, we might have strong consolation, who have fled for refuge to lay hold of the hope set before us.

—*Hebrews 6:17–18*

God is holy:

But as He who called you is holy, you also be holy in all your conduct, because it is written, "Be holy, for I am holy."

—*1 Peter 1:15–16*

God is love:

He who does not love does not know God, for God is love.

—*1 John 4:8*

God is spirit:

God is Spirit, and those who worship Him must worship in spirit and truth.

—*John 4:24*

No one has seen God at any time. The only begotten Son, who is in the bosom of the Father, He has declared Him.

—*John 1:18*

The Bible gives clear commands of how we ought to live our lives while on this earth. Many of the hundreds of commands for living can be seen throughout the books of Genesis, Exodus, Leviticus, Numbers, Deuteronomy, and beyond, and they can be summed up in a few Scriptural passages—one of which is found in two locations, which house what we know as the Ten Commandments.

The Ten Commandments is a list of religious and moral imperatives, a guide of sorts for moral behavior for the people of Israel. These instructions were spoken to Moses on Mount Sinai and given to him in the form of tablets. The Ten Commandments, as they have descriptively been named, became the moral foundation for the people of Israel. Consequently, they have also become the moral code for Christianity, Judaism, and Islam. The Ten Commandments serve as the moral foundation for our democracy in America and for Western civilization.

The Ten Commandments can be found in two locations in the Bible: Exodus 20:1–17 and Deuteronomy 5:6–21. Following is a synopsis of the typical way these commands are recounted.

- ✪ You shall have no other gods before me.
- ✪ You shall not make for yourself an idol.
- ✪ You shall not take the name of God in vain.
- ✪ Remember the Sabbath and keep it holy.
- ✪ Honor your father and mother.
- ✪ You shall not kill.

✪ You shall not commit adultery.

✪ You shall not steal.

✪ You shall not bear false witness against your neighbor.

✪ You shall not covet your neighbor's wife nor anything that belongs to your neighbor.

There are also two other commands that God gives, called the "Great Commandments". They are called this because the substance of all other commands or laws given by God rest on the principles given in the "Great Commandments".

Jesus said to him, "You shall love the Lord your God with all your heart, with all your soul, and with all your mind." This is the first and great commandment. And the second is like it: "You shall love your neighbor as yourself." On these two commandments hang all the Law and the Prophets.

—*Matthew 22:37–40*

Here, God tells us that our first duty is to love God. Our next order is to love our neighbor. Loving God and loving our neighbor is the key to living a Christian life. You cannot love God and simultaneously hate your neighbor. The two commandments go together. If you love God, you must love your neighbor.

God's major directives for life have come through a variety of interactions with God and humanity. These directives give clarity to how we are to live our lives on earth. There are many examples of God giving humankind directions concerning common practices for life—such as laws concerning diet, marriage, work, family, worship, relationships, war, and so on. Many of these laws were given to Moses as the leader of Israel. These laws, that give guidance to our day-to-day lives were given in times past and were accepted by the people as the norm for the children of Israel.

These laws and other holy-inspired writings and recordings of history have formed what we know as the Holy Scripture. These writings give us wisdom for living and a foundation for our faith.

Through the writings in both the Old and New Testament we get a basic understanding of the fundamentals of the Christian faith. The Bible presents a basic outline for understanding God, creation, sin, redemption, and Jesus Christ in relationship to God and humanity.

The following Fundamental Principles guide most Christian beliefs concerning the faith.

Fundamental Principle #1: God Is the Creator of All Things; There Is One God

Know therefore today, and take it to your heart, that the Lord, He is God in heaven above and on the earth below; there is no other.

—*Deuteronomy 4:39*

Remember the former things long past, for I am God, and there is no other; I am God, and there is no one like Me.

—*Isaiah 46:9*

In the beginning God created the heavens and the earth.

—*Genesis 1:1*

In the beginning was the Word, and the Word was with God, and the Word was God. He was in the beginning with God. All things were made through Him, and without Him nothing was made that was made.

—*John 1:1–3*

Fundamental Principle #2: Everyone Has Sinned and Is Separated from God

For all have sinned and fall short of the glory of God.

—*Romans 3:23*

But your iniquities have made a separation between you and your God, and your sins have hidden His face from you so that He does not hear.

—Isaiah 59:2

If we say that we have no sin, we deceive ourselves, and the truth is not in us. If we confess our sins, He is faithful and just to forgive us our sins and to cleanse us from all unrighteousness. If we say that we have not sinned, we make Him a liar, and His word is not in us.

—1 John 1:8–10

Fundamental Principle #3: There Is a Penalty for Sin

For the wages of sin is death, but the free gift of God is eternal life in Christ Jesus our Lord.

—Romans 6:23

And inasmuch as it is appointed for men to die once and after this comes judgment.

—Hebrews 9:27

But you, why do you judge your brother? Or you again, why do you regard your brother with contempt? For we will all stand before the judgment seat of God.

—Romans 14:10

These will go away into eternal punishment, but the righteous into eternal life.

—Matthew 25:46

Fundamental Principle #4: Jesus Paid the Penalty of Sin for All Who Believe In Him

But God demonstrates His own love toward us, in that while we were yet sinners, Christ died for us.

—Romans 5:8

For Christ also died for sins once for all, the just for the unjust, so that He might bring us to God, having been put to death in the flesh, but made alive in the spirit.

—*1 Peter 3:18*

All we like sheep have gone astray; we have turned, every one, to his own way; and the Lord has laid on Him the iniquity of us all.

—*Isaiah 53:6*

There is therefore now no condemnation to them which are in Christ Jesus.

—*Romans 8:1*

So Christ was offered once to bear the sins of many. To those who eagerly wait for Him He will appear a second time, apart from sin, for salvation.

—*Hebrews 9:28*

Fundamental Principle #5: No One Can Earn God's Forgiveness and Favor

For by grace you have been saved through faith; and that not of yourselves, it is the gift of God; not as a result of works, so that no one may boast.

—*Ephesians 2:8–9*

But when the kindness and the love of God our Savior toward man appeared, not by works of righteousness which we have done, but according to His mercy He saved us, through the washing of regeneration and renewing of the Holy Spirit,

—*Titus 3:4-5*

Fundamental Principle #6: We Can Have Assurance of God's Forgiveness

These things I have written to you who believe in the name of the Son of God, so that you may know that you have eternal life.

—*1 John 5:13*

In him we have redemption through his blood, the forgiveness of sins, in accordance with the riches of God's grace.

—*Ephesians 1:7*

For God so loved the world, that He gave His only begotten Son, that whoever believes in Him shall not perish, but have eternal life.

—*John 3:16*

As people of faith we can look at the very beginning of the Biblical account in the creation story. It is here that the Creator begins the process of establishing the world from animals, to plants, to humanity:

Then God said, "Let Us make man in Our image, according to Our likeness; let them have dominion over the fish of the sea, over the birds of the air, and over the cattle, over all the earth and over every creeping thing that creeps on the earth." So God created man in His own image; in the image of God He created him; male and female He created them.

—*Genesis 1.26–27*

Here we see that man and woman were made in the image and likeness of God. This tells us, both consciously and unconsciously, that all are made equal regardless of race, gender, or nation. This can be considered the beginning of the legal foundation that views all people as created equal and endowed by God with certain unfettered rights as stated in the Declaration of Independence. Likewise, this also becomes the foundation for the entirety of our legal system. This creation story in Genesis also assigns responsibility to humans for being caretakers of the earth that God had just created.

Humans are God's unique creations. As a special creation of God, humans were chosen to be stewards over all of creation. It is only through wisdom that humanity can be good stewards over what God has created. The Bible speaks extensively about the need for wisdom in our day-to-day lives. There is a difference between knowledge, information, and wisdom. Knowledge is derived from the collection of information and experiences. Wisdom is the ability to progressively apply knowledge in a relevant manner in our day to day lives. From a faith perspective, wisdom is the ability to use one's faith and make it relevant in our world as we know it.

Scripture has a lot to say about wisdom and its importance:

The fear of the Lord is the beginning of wisdom; a good understanding have all those who do His commandments. His praise endures forever.

—Psalm 111:10

To understand a proverb and an enigma, the words of the wise and their riddles. The fear of the Lord is the beginning of knowledge, but fools despise wisdom and instruction.

—Proverbs 1:6–8

My son, if you receive my words, And treasure my commands within you, So that you incline your ear to wisdom, And apply your heart to understanding; Yes, if you cry out for discernment, And lift up your voice for understanding, If you seek her as silver, And search for her as for hidden treasures; Then you will understand the fear of the Lord, And find the knowledge of God. For the Lord gives wisdom; From His mouth come knowledge and understanding; He stores up sound wisdom for the upright; He is a shield to those who walk uprightly; He guards the paths of justice, And preserves the way of His saints.

Then you will understand righteousness and justice, Equity and every good path.

—*Proverbs 2:1–9*

PROGRESSION OF POLICY

DEMOCRACY

(Chapter focus: Democracy)

◑

BELIEFS
(Chapter focus: What Would Jesus Do?)

Driven by:
Understanding Scripture

◑

IDEOLOGY

◑

POLICY

◑

POLITICS

CHAPTER SIX

What Would Jesus Do?

The Spirit of the Lord is upon Me, because He has anointed me to preach the gospel to the poor; He has sent me to heal the brokenhearted, to proclaim liberty to the captives and recovery of sight to the blind, to set at liberty those who are oppressed; to proclaim the acceptable year of the Lord.

—Luke 4:18–19

The opening Scripture of this chapter, Luke 4:18–19, can be a good lesson for political candidates, elected officials, and voters alike. Typically, candidates for office are good for making campaign promises or declarations of their beliefs. However, as actual elected officials, those promises made during the campaign trail are not always made into reality. Whereas when Jesus made certain statements about what He was called to do, he actually did what He said.

Inevitably, when we discuss matters of faith and how they are played out in our current world, many will ask the question: What Would Jesus Do? (WWJD). In order to best answer this question one must understand the characteristics of Jesus. We must truly understand who Jesus was and who he is in our present lives. Thus it is important to know, concerning Jesus, some of the following characteristics:

Jesus is fully God and fully man:

For in Him dwells all the fullness of the Godhead bodily; and you are complete in Him, who is the head of all principality and power.

—Colossians 2:9

For there is one God and one Mediator between God and men, the Man Christ Jesus.

—1 Timothy 2:5

Jesus was sinless:

For to this you were called, because Christ also suffered for us, leaving us an example, that you should follow His steps: "Who committed no sin, nor was deceit found in His mouth."

—1 Peter 2:21-22

Seeing then that we have a great High Priest who has passed through the heavens, Jesus the Son of God, let us hold fast our confession. For we do not have a High Priest who cannot sympathize with our weaknesses, but was in all points tempted as we are, yet without sin.

—Hebrews 4:14–15

Jesus is the only way to God the Father:

Jesus said to him, "I am the way, the truth, and the life. No one comes to the Father except through Me."

—John 14:6

So God created man in His own image; in the image of God He created him; male and female He created them.

—Genesis 1:27

Jesus died for the sins of each and every person in the world and paid the price for our sins:

My little children, these things I write to you, so that you may not sin. And if anyone sins, we have an Advocate with the Father, Jesus Christ the righteous. And He Himself is the propitiation for our sins, and not for ours only but also for the whole world.

—*1 John 2:1–2*

For the love of Christ compels us, because we judge thus: that if One died for all, then all died; and He died for all, that those who live should live no longer for themselves, but for Him who died for them and rose again.

—*2 Corinthians 5:14–15*

Who Himself bore our sins in His own body on the tree, that we, having died to sins, might live for righteousness—by whose stripes you were healed.

—*1 Peter 2:24*

Just as the Son of Man did not come to be served, but to serve, and to give His life a ransom for many.

—*Matthew 20:28*

Jesus answered and said to them, "Destroy this temple, and in three days I will raise it up." Then the Jews said, "It has taken forty-six years to build this temple, and will You raise it up in three days?" But He was speaking of the temple of His body. Therefore, when He had risen from the dead, His disciples remembered that He had said this to them, and they believed the Scripture and the word which Jesus had said.

—*John 2:19–22*

If you were to follow the basic principles of interpreting Scripture, you would first see what Jesus actually said. You would then begin interpreting what Jesus meant when he made his statements. You would conclude this process by determining how the original intent of Jesus message speaks to the current reality of our day. This is the process that will let you know as best as possible...what Jesus would do!

Although the task of knowing exactly how Jesus would act or think in modern times could be daunting, there are clues within scripture that inform us as to what Jesus would find important. Jesus gives us a hint in the proclamation call of his ministry. In Luke 4:18–19, Jesus repeats a statement given by the Prophet Isaiah of the Old Testament. Jesus, after being tempted by Satan for forty days, went to a synagogue in Nazareth, where he read the opening Scripture of this chapter (Luke 4:18–19) from the Book of Isaiah.

Jesus, in this passage, describes for his audience the details of his mission on the Earth. He states that his focus is on the poor, the brokenhearted, the captives, the blind, and the op-pressed. Jesus' focus was on those most vulnerable, those most in need, those whose voice had been muted by the world. So if you want to know what Jesus would do, start with what Jesus thought was important; start with what he spent the lion's share of his time dealing with. Jesus told everyone within the sound of his voice exactly what he felt he was called to do through his words. He then immediately took what he said he was called to do and made it a reality through his actions. What he said in words was authenticated by his actions. Jesus made these comments in the synagogue in front of a crowd of people. He made these statements to a group that was very skeptical about whether what he said was true or even possible. He stood before a crowd of people and made what can almost be described as a political promise. He immediately left and turned his words into actions. After he made these statements the people began questioning His authority and he fled to another town where he began doing exactly what he said he was called to do. Jesus literally traveled the land and preached the gospel, he healed people, and on and on. The following are examples of miracles Jesus performed immediately after his proclamation call in verses 18 and 19.

Now in the synagogue there was a man who had a spirit of an unclean demon. And he cried out with a loud voice, saying, "Let us alone! What have we to do with You, Jesus of Nazareth? Did You come to destroy us? I know who You are—the Holy One of God!" But Jesus rebuked him, saying, "Be quiet, and come out of him!" And when the demon had thrown him in their midst, it came out of him and did not hurt him.

—Luke 4:33-35

Now He arose from the synagogue and entered Simon's house. But Simon's wife's mother was sick with a high fever, and they made request of Him concerning her. So He stood over her and rebuked the fever, and it left her. And immediately she arose and served them.

—Luke 4:38–39

When the sun was setting, all those who had any that were sick with various diseases brought them to Him; and He laid His hands on every one of them and healed them. And demons also came out of many, crying out and saying, "You are the Christ, the Son of God!" And He, rebuking them, did not allow them to speak, for they knew that He was the Christ.

—Luke 4:40-41

Now when it was day, He departed and went into a deserted place. And the crowd sought Him and came to Him, and tried to keep Him from leaving them; but He said to them, "I must preach the kingdom of God to the other cities also, because for this purpose I have been sent." And He was preaching in the synagogues of Galilee.

—Luke 4:42-44

Jesus, in a teaching moment, gives us a clue as to what was of most importance to him. In what has been called the Beatitudes, Jesus says the following:

> *Blessed are the poor in spirit, For theirs is the kingdom of heaven. Blessed are those who mourn, For they shall be comforted. Blessed are the meek, For they shall inherit the earth. Blessed are those who hunger and thirst for righteousness, For they shall be filled. Blessed are the merciful, For they shall obtain mercy. Blessed are the pure in heart, For they shall see God. Blessed are the peacemakers, For they shall be called sons of God. Blessed are those who are persecuted for righteousness' sake, For theirs is the kingdom of heaven. Blessed are you when they revile and persecute you, and say all kinds of evil against you falsely for My sake. Rejoice and be exceedingly glad, for great is your reward in heaven, for so they persecuted the prophets who were before you.*

—Matthew 5.3-12

These verses talk about the hungry, lowly, the meek, the poor—basically, those most in need. Jesus calls all of these persons "blessed" despite their position or condition in life. As Jesus began his ministry, from the very outset he stated, "Repent, for the Kingdom of Heaven is at hand." As much as this was a spiritual statement, I believe it was also a political statement. At that time Herod Antipas was the ruler of Galilee, which was under the rule of the Roman Empire. Tiberius Caesar was the ruler of the Roman Empire at that time. I believe this statement was Jesus engaging the two rulers, Herod and Tiberius. When Jesus told the people to "repent," he was telling them to change their way of thinking. He was telling them to change what they had previously deemed important. The Kingdom of Heaven and what it represented was now important, not the King of Rome or of Galilee. The Kingdom of Heaven, as Jesus likely intended, was much different than the kingdoms of that day. It had nothing to do with the earthly kingdoms or kings of that day. It represented a set of ideals, a way of thinking about God and who God was in the lives of people. The terms "Kingdom of God" and "Kingdom of Heaven" can be used interchangeably. The book of Matthew is the only book in the Bible that uses the term "Kingdom of Heaven." The parallel Scriptures in the books of John, Luke, and Mark use the terms "Kingdom of God."

The Kingdom of Heaven and the Kingdom of God both represent God's rulership over the earth and its people. They represent God's omnipotence over the earth and its people. The will of God is reflected when Jesus prays in what we call the "Lord's Prayer." Here Jesus says, "Thy Kingdom come, Thy will be done on earth as it is in heaven" (Matthew 6:10). Jesus says the Kingdom of Heaven and the Kingdom of God is upon you, it is near you, and it is within you. Jesus called the people to be citizens of the Kingdom of God first and to live out their faith in every area of their lives. Jesus demonstrated this by what he devoted his time and energy to throughout the short span of his life. Jesus spoke to the "least of these"; he spoke to those who were frail (no sight, no hearing). He spoke to those with no hope, no money, and no home. Jesus tells us in Luke 4:18–19 what he was called to do and he spent the remainder of his life turning these words into reality.

We know that Jesus devoted the lion's share of his time and power on earth to the healing of the sick. This tells us that he was concerned about the sick. This means that Jesus would be concerned about sick people today. Although this might be a far stretch, I consider Jesus' concern for the sick to be a clue as to what would be important to him in today's society. I believe that Jesus would be concerned about the health care reform debate. We may not know what side of the political aisle of this subject matter he may align, but we do know that the end result would be to insure that America has a quality health care system for all Americans. We don't see in Scripture how Jesus would solve the issue, but we do know that he would be highly concerned about its outcome. This could cause many of us to believe that taking care of the sick should be priority on our list of political concerns.

The following are further examples, of whom and what Jesus found to be important. These persons were again those with limited means, resources and even intellectual capacity. These were people that had been taken advantage of or had been forgotten by society. These were people Jesus saw in the background and decidedly brought to the front to make them a viable part of society.

Jesus taught that the last will be first:

But many who are first will be last, and the last first.

—Matthew 19:30

Jesus' focus was on the least of these:

For I was hungry and you gave Me food; I was thirsty and you gave Me drink; I was a stranger and you took Me in; I was naked and you clothed Me; I was sick and you visited Me; I was in prison and you came to Me.

—Matthew 25:35–36

Jesus was humble and he taught humility:

For whoever exalts himself will be humbled, and he who humbles himself will be exalted.

—Luke 14:11

Jesus spoke in parables when speaking to his audience. Jesus used these parables to teach important messages to those who listened. We can also use these parables to see what was of high importance to Jesus.

Parable—The Rich Man & Lazarus:

There was a certain rich man who was clothed in purple and fine linen and fared sumptuously every day. But there was a certain

beggar named Lazarus, full of sores, who was laid at his gate, de-
siring to be fed with the crumbs which fell from the rich man's table.
Moreover the dogs came and licked his sores. So it was that the
beggar died, and was carried by the angels to Abraham's bosom.
The rich man also died and was buried. And being in torments
in Hades, he lifted up his eyes and saw Abraham afar off, and
Lazarus in his bosom. Then he cried and said, "Father Abraham,
have mercy on me, and send Lazarus that he may dip the tip of
his finger in water and cool my tongue; for I am tormented in this
flame." But Abraham said, "Son, remember that in your lifetime
you received your good things, and likewise Lazarus evil things; but
now he is comforted and you are tormented."

—Luke 16:19–25

Moral of the story: Jesus places highest priority to those with
limited means, even over those who have great means! Jesus is
concerned about the "least of these".

Parable—The Lost Sheep

What do you think? If a man has a hundred sheep, and one of
them goes astray, does he not leave the ninety-nine and go to the
mountains to seek the one that is straying? And if he should find
it, assuredly, I say to you, he rejoices more over that sheep than
over the ninety-nine that did not go astray. Even so it is not the
will of your Father who is in heaven that one of these little ones
should perish.

—Matthew 18:12–14

Moral of the story: Jesus is concerned about all of God's
children. Even if one is gone astray, God will focus on the one in
order to save them.

Jesus in Scripture can be seen in two different lights. He typically is seen as a personal savior. As shown in Scripture, Jesus was
born to die sacrificially for the sins of all humanity. Throughout
the belief system of Christianity it is taught that Jesus was sent to

the earth to die for the sins of the world, that those who believe would have everlasting life. Jesus can also be seen as social activist. Jesus, in this light, is one who fights in the name of what is right, in the name of justice for those who are in need. When Jesus is viewed as personal savior, it focuses the belief of the individual on personal holiness, a call to personal piety and salvation. Jesus as social activist, however, directs the belief of the individual toward social holiness, a call to social action. As I see it, we must proclaim both sides of the Gospel of Jesus Christ in order to truly live out a life that is in concert with the life of Jesus. We must live a life that promotes personal piety. We must also live a life that promotes social action towards justice and righteousness.

Jesus as personal savior is connected to the "Great Command", when it says to love God. Jesus as personal activist is connected to the "Great Command", when it says to love thy neighbor. To love God and to love thy neighbor describes the different aspects of Jesus. Both aspects of Jesus and the "Great Command" must be acted out in all that we do in our lives. Jesus was concerned about His relationship with the Father, but He was equally concerned about His connection and work for the people of God.

PROGRESSION OF POLICY

DEMOCRACY

Ŏ

BELIEFS

Driven by:
Family Values, Faith in God, Understanding Scripture

Ŏ

IDEOLOGY
(Chapter focus: Ideology)

Ŏ

POLICY

Ŏ

POLITICS

CHAPTER SEVEN

Ideology—What is it and How Do You Develop It?

It is written, Man shall not live by bread alone, but by every word that proceeds from the mouth of God.

—Matthew 4:4

Politics is stocked full of strong ideas and strong personalities. Politics is packed with opinionated people who feel passionately about their perspectives on people, politics, and public policy. Personal perspectives and ideas are the main drivers for political movements, parties, and public policy. A person's political position originates from their basic beliefs concerning humanity and their view of people and the world. It can be likened to the tip of an iceberg. What people espouse as their political position is only the outgrowth of a much larger belief and thought process (see diagram).

It is ideology that drives the political world. Whether it's personal ideology or whether it's simply an adopted one from a particular individual or group, it is the ideologies of people that make the political world go round. Thus the first step in setting your own political compass is to develop your personal ideology.

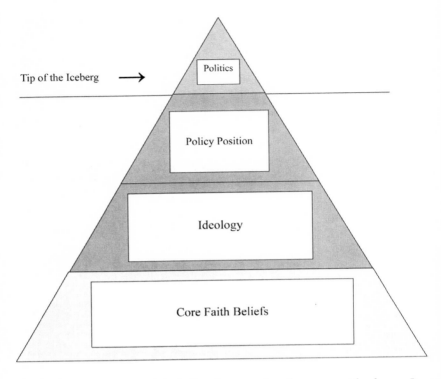

It takes real work and dedication to develop your ideology. It takes having a basic understanding of what you believe on a whole host of topics that will help you to define your personal ideology.

Political ideology concerns itself with issues such as the role of government, health care, criminal justice, foreign policy, fiscal policy, education, military defense, the environment, social welfare, social security, transportation, and tax policy, just to name a few. A person's ideological viewpoint generally dictates the direction of his or her political and policy positions.

You are likely asking the big question: What is an ideology? The definition of "ideology" is the body of ideas reflecting the social needs and aspirations of an individual, group, class, or culture. It is a set of doctrines or beliefs that form the basis of a political, economic, or philosophical system. An ideology is a collection of ideas. Typically these ideologies contain ideas that speak to the best form of government to fulfill those ideals. Political parties base their actions and programs on ideologies. A politically based ideology concerns itself with the allocation of power and resources in the world of government.

The question now remains—how does one develop one's own personal ideology? How does one develop a set of beliefs that will ultimately form the basis for a personal political ideology? How is one's personal belief system developed? Is it developed through nurture or nature? Is one's belief system naturally developed through birth, or is it determined because of the nurturing of one's environment through family, friends, or institutions in one's life?

I submit that one's value system is developed by what one cherishes the most. For some, what is cherished most is their belief in people or their belief in country. For many, what is cherished the most is their belief and faith in God. For those in this number, faith in God serves as a guide for the majority of life's issues. My personal ideology is formed as a result of my personal belief in God. It is therefore that personal belief in God that informs my personal ideology, which then informs my personal political ideology.

One of the previous questions posed is whether one's ideology is developed via nature or nurture. I will submit that it is a combination of the two. I believe that we all have a certain level of God consciousness that, rightfully so, brings a belief and connection to God. In the creation story, as referenced in the introduction of this book, God, when he created humans, made them in His own image (Genesis 1:26–27). While being in the image of God does not make us God, it does give us a certain connection with the Creator. Thus it is inevitable that a certain part of people's ideology is formed simply because of the God consciousness within each of us.

However, I believe the greatest influence over our value system is through nurture. This means that something within our en-

Faith in God

=

Personal understanding and relationship with God

◖◗

Personal Idealogy

=

Set of doctrines or beliefs derived from Faith in God

◖◗

Personal Political Idealogy

=

Set of political doctrines or beliefs derived from Personal Idealogy

vironment tangibly influences the outcome of our personality, character, or behavior. The people who hold the greatest influence over our life, for better or for worse, are our parents. It is the parents who teach children the foundational things of life: how to eat, how to speak, how to learn, how to think, and on and on and on! Parents are the primary reason why children succeed or fail in school and/or in life. Thus what one holds to be true or values the most is heavily influenced by one's family and upbringing. The Bible confirms this reality when it commands us all to "train a child in the way he should go, and when he is old he will not turn from it" (Proverbs 22:6).

Your ideology, your set of beliefs, is developed as a result of gathering various points of view, various perspectives, and creating a set of thoughts that inform your world (in this case the world of politics). From a faith perspective, your ideology is developed by gathering information and developing various points of view through your interpretation of Scripture. The wisdom, stories, parables, letters, and general writings of the Bible all give clues as to what God holds to be good and true. For the layperson, let's briefly discuss the Bible. The Bible is a collection of books accepted by Christians as the sacred Holy Scripture, divinely inspired by God. These books provide the basis for our beliefs concerning God, Jesus and, spiritual matters. They provide us with guiding principles for morality and moral living.

Crafting a set of beliefs that is both relevant to public policy and also informed by one's faith perspective can be a daunting task. One must be able to digest Scripture and translate it in a manner that is meaningful to inform one's life. In order to have and develop an ideology that is true to your faith, you must have a good understanding of the basic tenets of the faith. It is difficult to understand the more complex components of the faith if the general principles of Scripture are not well understood. We must live our life through the lens of these basic tenets when determining how we ought to behave in our daily lives. Scripture, thus, must be seen by its readers as being the authentic Word of God that holds tremendous power. Essentially, the authenticity of Scripture is validated by one's personal relationship with God. If one truly believes that the Scripture "*is* given by inspiration of God" (2 Timothy 3:16)—then what it says should also be valuable to inform one's personal ideology.

A good exercise to help define your ideology, from a faith perspective, is to develop a list of issues. Once you have a good list of issues on paper, ask yourself: "What do I believe the Bible says in relationship to these issues?" What does the Bible say regarding this issue or what overall principle does the Bible espouse that can speak relevantly to this issue? In cases where the Bible doesn't speak directly concerning a subject matter, look for stories, parables, wisdom anecdotes, or biblical descriptions of history in relationship to your issue. Once you have identified various Scriptures that in some way speak to these issues, the tough work begins.

It is very reasonable to say that our belief in God, our understanding of Scripture, can and should have an influence over our day-to-day lives. This also means that our faith can and should have an influence on our policies and politics. Remember, the separation of church and state is only relevant where the institution of the church and the institution of the government are concerned. It never negates our ability to allow our faith to influence our policies. As long as our policies don't infringe on the rights of others, then our faith should have an impact on policies that we espouse.

The question then arises, how does Scripture play out in developing our stance on public policy? How do I take an ancient document that spoke to the culture and times of that period and make it relevant to the culture and times of this present age? Part of the answer for these questions relies heavily on one's understanding and interpretation of Scripture. Although this book is not geared toward helping you understand Scripture or even toward how to approach Scripture; so much of your understanding of Scripture will rest on how you actually engage the text. There are techniques and approaches to Scripture that are helpful in getting a more complete understanding of matters of faith in Scripture. Although we won't go into great detail regarding this, there are ways to understand Scripture that will simplify the text and add to your understanding regarding its meaning. When reading Scripture, here are some simple exercises to consider that may help in your understanding and interpretation of the text:

- ✪ What does this passage say?
- ✪ What does this passage mean?
- ✪ To what socio-political-economic issue does this passage speak?
- ✪ How can I apply the meaning of this passage to develop my ideological position?

Religions have risen and fallen on the backs of poorly crafted interpretations of Scripture. People live their lives based on their personal interpretations of Scripture. Church denominations and groups have been created based on what readers believed were the "true" meanings behind the text in the Bible. Cults and fringe religious groups thrive on the backs of narrowly developed views of Scripture. Therefore, the difficult work begins in the actual interpretation of the writing itself. Applying a method of interpretation to passages of Scripture can be a very difficult, intimidating, and time-consuming task.

C.S. Lewis states, concerning the interpretation of Scripture, "Look. Listen. Receive." This is an important phrase to retain. When thinking about interpretation one should first *look* at the Scripture. This means to simply read the text of the Scripture. As simple as this may sound, no truth can come through the Bible if people of faith don't begin with this most simple task. Reading is fundamental! Look at what the text is referencing. Look for the contextual setting of the verse(s). Look at where it lies within the

Bible; is it in the Old or New Testament? Is it written by Jesus, prophets, kings . . . is it a song, poem, or parable? Look to see who wrote the text and how it is written. Once the reading of the text takes place, read it again. This time while you are reading the text, *listen* to what it is saying! Listen to what it is referencing in its Scripture. Listen for hidden meanings. Listen for allegorical stories, listen for metaphors in the story, and listen for contrast and comparisons.

Then, once you have exhaustively listened to the text, *receive*. One must receive all that the Scripture has to say on a matter, concerning life, concerning our relationship with God, concerning our relationship with all of humanity and the earth. You must receive so that the meaning that is within the Scriptures is brought to life.

There are three components within Bible interpretation that can be used to determine the meaning of certain passages. They are the author, the reader, and the text itself. Somehow the reader must efficiently gain from the text what the author meant when he or she wrote it and somehow bring meaning out of the text to speak to our modern situations. Simply put, the text is solid; it means what the writer originally intended it to mean. It is our job to figure out what that original meaning was and use it to apply it to our daily situations. The full process of interpretation can be overwhelming, but relax—there are many Bible tools out there that can assist a person during their process of interpretation, such as Bible commentaries, Bible dictionaries, Bible handbooks, and so on.

When reading Scripture, we must pay attention to the context. The reader must look at the context of the Scripture in many ways.

Textual Context

One aspect of looking at Scriptural context is through the actual text itself. When undergoing the process of biblical interpretation, one must look at the context of the text. A word on its own may or may not mean what we think it does. Many words have multiple meanings and are only adequately defined within the context of the sentence or paragraph in which it resides. Likewise, when interpreting verses of Scripture, a verse may not mean what originally was thought when read within the context of the chapter and book in which it resides. A good practice in interpreting Scripture is to first read the actual verse of Scripture in question. Next, read the verse prior to and following the verse in question. The next step is to read the entire chapter. Finally, read the entire book if time permits. This will give the reader a better perspective on what was going on within the context of the entire writing itself.

Historical Context

When reading Scripture one must know what was going on historically during the time of the writing. The reader must, as best as possible, understand the historical background of the text. Understanding the historical context of that time may add value to the interpretation process. It is good to know what the writers and receivers of the messages were experiencing during that moment in history. Understanding things such as the state of the economy or foreign relations of that time period is helpful information when interpreting the Scriptures in question.

Situational Context

Who is the audience? Who is listening or reading the letter? These are helpful things to know when interpreting Scripture. It is important to clearly define the audience that is receiving the message. Questions such as whether there is a live audience or whether the audience is simply reading the message from a penned letter are also important. Is the passage communicated orally or written? Knowing the location of the messenger during the reception of the message is helpful. Understanding if the messenger is speaking in a synagogue, on the street, at a house, or in a field are all good questions to be asked and answered inside the text.

One must also understand the different types of literature for which a passage can be written. There are various forms of literature by which Bibles passages were written. Understanding the form in which each passage of Scripture was written will help give greater clarity to the reading of the passage. Below are types of literature in the Bible.

Bible Narratives

Narratives are of the largest types of writing in the Bible. The Bible is comprised of many small narratives or stories that fit within the context of a much larger narrative within the chapters, books, and Old and New Testaments. It is important to understand each narrative within the context of larger narrative perspectives. Narratives are the telling of stories. The Bible is stocked full of stories initially presented orally, then finally put down in written form. These stories serve to present historical events, real and created stories, and much more in an effort to convey messages and principles to its readers.

Letters or Epistles

Much of the writing of the Apostle Paul is written in the form of letters or epistles. Paul, in many of his letters, is either writing to individuals (i.e. Timothy, Titus, or Philemon) or to cities or groups of people (i.e. Corinthians, Galatians, or Ephesians). It is important to understand within these letters whom they were written to, whom they were written about, or even why they were written.

Parables

Jesus spoke heavily in parables. Parables are simple stories, generally fictional in nature, that illustrate moral lessons for its listeners. The format for most of the parables that Jesus told would begin with the telling of the story followed immediately by an explanation of its meaning. The purpose of these parables was to teach real life lessons through, fictional stories and characters.

Wisdom

Ecclesiastes and Proverbs are books filled with points of wisdom almost from the beginning of the books to the end. There are other books, such as Psalms and Song of Solomon, that include major wisdom writings as well. These are writings that are meant to teach lessons in small, bite-size increments or within the context of stories—true or hypothetical. These pieces of wisdom can be used as a guideline for everyday living.

Hyperbole

Hyperbole is written throughout the entirety of the Bible. Ironically, many Christians may not want to highly publicize the fact that hyperbole is present in scripture, given the fact that there are many who seek to discredit the authenticity of the Bible. However, this form of literature also has a purpose for its readers. Exaggeration is a unique method to make a definitive point within the context of the story. This type of literature is important to highlight because there are many examples of hyperbole in Scripture, and you must be able to distinguish hyperbole from factual stories. Hyperbole is used to provide a very pointed effect throughout its message.

Poetry

Almost a third of the Old Testament is written in poetry. The poetry in the Old Testament is not as concerned about rhythm and rhyme as it is in our modern usage of poetry. Old Testament poetry uses what is called parallelism. This is where lines or verses of Scripture are repeated or contrasted by the next line in order to fully highlight the meaning of the original verse itself. The reader should be able to recognize poetry in writings since poetry, to some degree, is illustrated by the use of emotions in its message.

The accurate interpretation of scripture should be priority number one within Christianity. In order to accurately interpret Scripture we must have an authentic and valid method of deciphering it. The process for interpreting Scripture is called Hermeneutics. When interpreting Scripture to gain wisdom for our present-day lives we must, in some way, make that interpretation relevant to our modern-day world. We must interpret Scripture first to find the original meaning of the text. The process for the interpretation of Scripture's original meaning is called Exegesis. Before finding meaning that speaks to our current-day situation, one must understand what the writer intended when he or she wrote it. Once there is a good grasp of the original meaning of the text, the process of bringing real life relevance of the Scripture can begin. Attempting to find relevance of Scripture in our modern times is called Exposition. When we read Scripture to overlay its original meaning to our current life situation, we are "Receiving" from Scripture.

As C.S. Lewis stated in regards to interpreting Scripture, we must Look, Listen, and Receive. The first two actions, "Look" and "Listen," are used primarily in the exegesis of Scripture. The action "Receive" is what is used to graft the original meaning of the text onto our modern-day understanding of issues. When people read Scripture, they do so mostly to get a better understanding of their Christian faith. It helps to explain, as best as can be, why we believe what we believe. The tendency when reading the Bible is to first read the text and immediately attempt to give meaning to our everyday situation. However, to make this leap first would be premature. The first step in gaining a modern-day understanding of Scripture is to first determine its original meaning as the author intended it. We must also, to the best of our ability, determine the hearer's or readers' interpretation of that message as it was received at that time. Once the exegesis process is completed and a good understanding of its original meaning is ascertained, one can then begin the process of exposition. You must take first things first.

The Bible offers many opportunities to gain wisdom concerning life's issues. The engagement of Scripture with real-world issues can be done either through a direct or indirect approach of Scripture. For example, an issue concerning a topic may be handled directly in Scripture because the topic itself was directly referenced. This is the easy way of interpreting Scripture. It makes the interpretation process much simpler when an issue is directly referenced within Scripture and dealt with. A good example of this is through the examples of parables. There are many parables given by Jesus that talk about certain issues and name them by name. In this scenario, Jesus communicates the parable, and then explains its meaning. Here, Jesus makes the process of interpretation much easier by the direct approach. The more difficult proposition in Scripture is to develop an understanding on a matter that the Bible is silent. The question then remains—if the Bible is silent on a subject matter, how can you develop a position from a Christian perspective?

A superior understanding of the Bible will help believers of the faith shed light on those silent areas of the Bible. By having a thorough understanding of the Bible and its writings, characters, and history, we allow a greater opportunity to make it more relevant toward our daily lives. Even when a matter is not addressed in Scripture, there are still learning opportunities based upon what we do know and understand of Scripture as a whole. We must learn to read and correctly interpret Scripture before we can connect any modern-day meaning. The following brief outline gives a basic overview of what the interpretation process looks like.

Hermeneutics = process of Interpretation

First Step: Exegesis

⇓

Second Step: Exposition

Hermaneutics Revisited

In order to understand Scripture we must undertake the process of hermeneutics by first employing the process of exegesis. This will empower us to find the original meaning of the text. We must then do an exposition of the Scripture's text to allow for a relevancy of meaning for our lives today. Exegesis, as the first order of biblical interpretation, is essential in developing an informed ideology that is guided by the Christian faith. One must have at least a basic knowledge of Scripture in its totality to have an informed faith. Exegesis is the first step of knowing and understanding Scripture as the precursor to a proper interpretation of the text.

Understanding the context of Scripture is fundamental to a good evaluation of the text you are studying. Understanding the context of the text itself or the context of the history, culture, or language of the time is an asset for full interpretation of Scripture. One word in isolation has limited meaning within itself. However, when read in the context of a sentence, a paragraph, a chapter, or an entire book, that word comes alive and greater meaning of that word can be realized. Likewise, a verse of Scripture has only limited meaning on its own, but when read in the context of an entire chapter, book, or the entire canon of Scripture, the full meaning of Scripture can be brought to life.

Remember the goal of exegesis is to find the original intent of Scripture as it was written in its time. That being said, understanding the historical backdrop of the Scripture in question is very important in understanding its original intent. Understanding the cultural happenings, economic situation, foreign and domestic situations of that time is important. When understanding any writings or literary work, we can't help but read it through the lens of our modern view of the world. Thus, by understanding the historical background of the passage in question, the reader will be able to gain a greater understanding of the original intent of the writing and the writer. It allows the reader to somehow transfer him or herself into the times of the writing so that the intent of the writer can be heard as clearly as possible.

The process of exegesis and exposition is what gives true clarity to our ideology—ah, there's that word again. The premise of this book says that our faith should be intricately woven throughout the fabric of our lives. Many Christians build their faith largely on the interpretation and understanding of the Bible. Thus, once a basic overview of how to interpret Scripture is completed, one must determine how the interpretation of Scripture, both on an exegetical and expository level, works to form one's ideological perspective.

Once the full engagement of Scripture is settled, the process to merge one's understanding of the Bible with public policy issues begins. So the question remains, how do I develop my ideology in a manner that is true to my faith perspective? The question is a valid one, but we must be conscious of the fact that it takes time to develop your ideology. It takes time and effort to realize a well developed ideology. It takes constant interaction with the Bible as a whole. It takes a concerted effort to develop your faith perspective. We must remember that our ideology is inextricably connected to our interpretation of Scripture. Thus we must engage Scripture directly and often.

The following are helpful exercises to undertake when attempting to connect policies to Scripture. These exercises can be used to effectively form a bridge between policy and actual Bible references.

Exercises:

- ✪ Develop a list of issues or topics that are generally debated in government. *(Examples: health care, social welfare, education, the economy, foreign policy, defense, the environment, etc.)*
- ✪ Write down everything that may be in Scripture that is pertinent to that issue or topic, whether directly or indirectly.
- ✪ Determine how the totality of Scripture relates to the topic at hand. *(This is when you implement the process of interpretation as previously highlighted.)*

PROGRESSION OF POLICY

DEMOCRACY

⇓

BELIEFS

Driven by:
Family Values, Faith in God, Understanding Scripture

⇓

IDEOLOGY

⇓

POLICY
(Chapter focus: From Idealogy to Policy)

⇓

POLITICS

CHAPTER EIGHT

From Ideology to Policy

My brethren, do not hold the faith of our Lord Jesus Christ, the Lord of glory, with partiality. For if there should come into your assembly a man with gold rings, in fine apparel, and there should also come in a poor man in filthy clothes, and you pay attention to the one wearing the fine clothes and say to him, "You sit here in a good place," and say to the poor man, "You stand there," or, "Sit here at my footstool," have you not shown partiality among yourselves, and become judges with evil thoughts? Listen, my beloved brethren: Has God not chosen the poor of this world to be rich in faith and heirs of the kingdom which He promised to those who love Him? But you have dishonored the poor man. Do not the rich oppress you and drag you into the courts? Do they not blaspheme that noble name by which you are called?

—*James 2.1–7*

The scripture above speaks about giving priority to the poor over the rich. It tells us that if our faith speaks to giving attention to those in need, then our actions ought to follow suit. The scripture speaks to the historical tendency of giving special attention to the rich. However, our faith tells us to do just the opposite. Therefore, making your faith a reality means giving special attention not to the rich, but to those most in need...the poor.

The question remains, how does one make the leap from personal beliefs to policy? How do you translate what you believe into policy? How do you take what you believe, translate it into your own political position, and use it to influence the actions of our nation and government? The easiest way to accomplish this is to take one issue at a time and determine what your basic position is for each issue. Let's take four different types of policies and talk about what the Bible might say both directly and indirectly concerning them. Let's deal with social policy, foreign policy, criminal justice policy, and environmental policy.

Social Policy

Social policy deals with basic human welfare and seeks to address specific areas such as education, health, housing, social security, and so on. Social policy concerns itself not with equality but with equity. The term "equal" deals with being of the same measure, quantity, or amount. The term "equity" deals with simply being fair or unbiased. Social policy is concerned with the basic welfare of all its citizens. Thus when one is talking about the welfare of the people, it may look different for different people. Social policy concerning education may simply say that all citizens have the right to a proper education. However, this right may not offer the same opportunities for every person or community. Society has shown us that schools and school districts are not all created equal. They may all provide an education for its citizens, but the quality of that education may not be equal. One school within a district may have a passing mark academically while another within that same district may be failing. A social policy concerning education may place more resources within the failing school. It may appear unfair to put more money in one school over another. It may seem unfair to use a special curriculum to address the unique and unmet needs of one student body over another. It may seem unfair to treat one school different than another but it is all in the name of equity. It is offering a fair opportunity for all kids to have a proper education, not just those who live in certain communities or zip codes.

James 2:1–7 talks about not giving special attention to the wealthy. It actually shows how God has a special concern and love for the poor and those in need. The Bible gives a good amount of direction regarding who should receive extra help and assistance. The Bible tells its readers to help the poor, the needy, the hungry, the captive, the widowed, and the children, to name a few. This Scripture can and probably has been used to direct social policy. This Scripture clearly directs us to give special attention to the poor, not just to the rich.

The first goal when dealing with social policy should be to assist those most in need. The next goal should be to help them become self-sufficient. Without stating support for or against any particular policy or legislation, I will say that what I personally look for in policy is how it affects the "least of these." Does it really provide assistance? Does it really help those most in need? Does it give them a much-needed hand up in the world? Does it really offer them an opportunity to be self sufficient, meaning will it equip them to not have to use this assistance again.

Social policy should empower the benefactors of the policy. At the end of the day we must have a government that creates a reasonable environment for life, liberty, and the pursuit of happiness for its citizens. Social policy should create a vehicle by which those most in need can create a life of self-sufficiency. Social policy should never be used to simply care for those unwilling to work or provide for themselves.

Therefore, when we talk about helping the poor and the least of these, as referenced in James 2:1–4; we must do so in the light of 2 Thessalonians 3:10 when it states, "If anyone will not work, neither shall he eat." In order to serve the poor through policy, we must do so through the lens of personal responsibility. For every policy topic you should be able to overlay your faith perspective through Scripture in order to give the everyday citizen a faith-based mechanism to have one's faith inform one's politics.

Let's consider a clear policy position from time's past. The Department of Housing and Urban Development (HUD) offers many programs designed to assist citizens most in need. One such program is the Section 8 Voucher Program. Its purpose is to assist eligible low-income households by paying a portion of the rent to the owners/landlords. Its intent is to assist individuals and families to reside in decent, safe, and sanitary rental housing. This program was established to help people who have little to no resources provide housing for themselves. This is a type of social policy.

HUD was established when President Lyndon B. Johnson signed the HUD Act into law in 1965. This law was a part of a sweeping program of laws as a part of his Great Society plan, which was championed by President Johnson to eliminate poverty and to fight racial injustices. This program addressed a number of issues of the day, including education, medical care, transportation and urban issues. Major funding was established to adequately address these issues as well. It is important to note that the HUD Act and the Great Society program are forms of social policy.

In all of our policy or political deliberations there are budgetary implications that follow and guide its implementation. Many politicians use the budget to hide behind their true positions concerning various policies. Luke 12:34 says, "For where your treasure is, there your heart will be also." Your heart can be likened to your policy choices, whereas your treasure is likened to your financial decisions. Dr. Martin Luther King, Jr. stated it another way. He said, "A nation that continues year after year to spend more money on military defense than on programs of social uplift is a nation approaching spiritual death." What's of equal importance concerning one's policy position is not the position itself, but the action that supports one's position. A policy issue is powerless if not supported by the necessary funding to make it a reality. For example, political candidates and elected officials for decades have stated that they are in support of affordable access to health care for all Americans. However, these statements were primarily useless, because the corresponding resources were never put in place to make this a reality.

Therefore, it is safe to say that the hundreds, maybe even thousands, of U.S. Representatives, Senators, Governors, and Presidents over the span of history did not, as a collective body, really ever support comprehensive health care reform because they were not ready to fund it. This can be likened to the Scripture that says, "Faith without works is dead" (James 2:20). Thus, people's words must match their deeds. This should be the measuring stick for whether an elected official is doing what he or she says that he or she would do. The measuring stick for all elected officials should be whether their words match their deeds.

Foreign Policy

Romans 12:17–21 tells us, "Repay no evil for evil." It gives a somewhat different understanding of relating to our enemies or relating to those who do evil to us. It tells us to actually help our enemy:

> *Repay no one evil for evil. Have regard for good things in the sight of all men. If it is possible, as much as depends on you, live peaceably with all men. Beloved, do not avenge yourselves, but rather give place to wrath; for it is written, "Vengeance is Mine, I will repay," says the Lord. Therefore, "If your enemy is hungry, feed him; If he is thirsty, give him a drink; for in so doing you will heap coals of fire on his head. Do not be overcome by evil, but overcome evil with good." (Romans 12:17–21)*

This Scripture tells us to befriend opposing forces, to get close with our enemies. This is completely counter to what our culture says is appropriate for dealing with our enemies. Most people separate from their enemies so as not to be hurt by them. However, this Scripture tells us to feed our enemies when they are hungry and to give them drink when they are thirsty. Something to consider in this scenario is that in order to give food for the hungry, drink for the thirsty and clothing for the naked, one must physically be in close proximity to the people so as to know what their needs are. I believe the deeper wisdom of this Scripture is that we must open lines of communication with our enemy in order to resolve any conflicts that may exist. Concerning public policy, this can also be a directive on how to deal with our "enemies." This Scripture can be used to inform our foreign policy. This Scripture tells us that we must keep lines of communication open with our friends and foes internationally. The clearer the lines of communication across international lines, the better our international relationships will be.

Criminal Justice Policy

Let's be clear that those who break the laws of our society, especially those of a felonious nature, can be considered enemies of the state. However, instead of killing our enemies, Scripture is asking us to care for them. This is a very difficult teaching to accept, but it takes some serious consideration to really understand what this Scripture really means in our daily lives.

Galatians 6:1–2 tells us to restore those who have been caught up in trespasses: "Brethren, if a man is overtaken in any trespass, you who are spiritual restore such a one in a spirit of gentleness, considering yourself lest you also be tempted. Bear one another's burdens, and so fulfill the law of Christ."

Essentially, this passage tells us to work to restore those persons who sin or who have committed some type of trespass. "Restore" means to bring back to or put back into a former or original state. Thus based on these and other Scriptures, we must ask ourselves, what does the Judeo-Christian tradition say about our criminal justice system? This nation's method of handling our criminal justice system is one that seeks to punish according to the corresponding crime. It is a system of retributive justice, one that says, "If you do the crime, you do the time." It seems to believe that a heavy punitive form of criminal justice is the way to keep the public safe. I would submit that the Judeo-Christian faith promotes restorative justice, not retributive justice. Restorative justice focuses on rehabilitation first. It places priority on the transformation of the criminal in order to truly reduce recidivism. This priority, however, has to be met with a healthy dose of caution, because government's first responsibility is for the public safety of its citizens. There must be a balance between the desires to transform public offenders against the mission to protect the public's safety.

Environmental Policy

There are many Scriptures that deal with God giving humans the ability to have dominion and control over creation. One is Genesis 1:1–2: "In the beginning God created the heavens and the earth. The earth was without form, and void; and darkness was on the face of the deep. And the Spirit of God was hovering over the face of the waters."

These verses tell us that in the very beginning the world was formless until God began the great creation event, as spelled out in the book of Genesis. As the first verse reads, God created the "heavens and the earth." Later, in Genesis 1:26, God creates man and woman (Adam and Eve) and gives them the responsibilities over all of creation: "Then God said, Let Us make man in Our image, according to Our likeness; let them have dominion over the fish of the sea, over the birds of the air, and over the cattle, over all the earth and over every creeping thing that creeps on the earth."

God goes even further by giving Adam and Eve more responsibility over creation in Genesis 2:19: "Out of the ground the Lord God formed every beast of the field and every bird of the air, and brought them to Adam to see what he would call them. And whatever Adam called each living creature that was its name."

In these verses of Scripture God not only gives humanity the responsibility of being a good steward over the earth, He also gives them the responsibility of naming all of God's creations. I interpret these Scriptures as a call to action in the protection of the environment as our God-given responsibility. Thus, it is our responsibility as citizens to protect the environment through our actions, practices, and policies.

The start of your journey to connect Scripture with public policy begins with the engagement of your faith and of Scripture. It ends with your understanding of both Scripture and of politics. Once there is a basic understanding of both Scripture and politics, you must now build a bridge from one to the other. This begins with the hermeneutical process: Exegesis and Exposition. We must first ascertain the original intent of the Scripture. We must then take the original meaning as laid out in Scripture and overlay its current-day meaning for our present-day life. Once we have some level of interpretation of Scripture based upon our analysis, we then must connect it with public policy issues.

Ideology to policy is much like the Scripture verse concerning faith and works. Ideology is to faith as policy is to works. Both ideology and faith speak of a belief system that remains theoretical until something turns that theory into reality. Both policy and works are the realization of the theoretical stance or position one may hold.

It is important to remember that an ideology is simply a set of beliefs that form a foundation for a given system. In the case of politics, one's ideology is the set of beliefs or ideas that eventually give direction to government. It is these set of beliefs that help determine one's stance on foreign policy, on tax policy, on the environment, on the economy, and so on. It is ideology that drives policy in the direction that actual governance ought to go.

Concerning candidates for office, we must look beyond the superficial aspects of a candidate, such as looks, personality, race, age, and so on; we must look at and inquire about what the candidate truly believes. It is only after we have a greater understanding of their belief system that we will be empowered to make a truly informed decision regarding our vote for a candidate for elected office.

Many say that knowledge is power; however, I disagree with that statement—it is *applied* knowledge that is power! Information alone is only words, text, and ideas. Advocacy is defined as the act or process of advocating or supporting a cause, proposal, or interests of another. Like previous references made to James 2:20, advocacy is like the verse that says, "Faith without works is dead." Faith alone, as Scripture states, is like a man saying to a homeless man, "Be ye warmed or be ye fed." Likewise, faith is like ideology and advocacy is like works. It really doesn't matter what you believe, if you are not willing to put your beliefs into action! If you don't step forward and make known what you believe through your actions, then you are saying that you are satisfied with the status quo. Your silence says that you are satisfied with the present state of our society. Advocacy allows you to make known what you believe on any given subject or issue.

The civil rights movement would have never been a "movement" without a group of people holding a set of beliefs that protected the human rights of all people. This movement innately believed that "all men are created equal" and were "endowed by the Creator with certain unalienable rights." These beliefs for many were supported by their Christian faith. This perspective informed them that God was the creator of all humanity, that God was a God of liberation. They believed in the same God that freed the children of Israel from the oppression of the Egyptian people. It was their belief that Jesus Christ came to free people of their bondage of sin through the sacrifice of His life on Calvary. The people of the civil rights movement used these examples and their understanding of God and Scripture to form their ideology. It was this ideology that eventually translated into the revocation of Jim Crow laws. It was this ideology that translated into the passage of the Civil Rights Act (1964) and the Voting Rights Act (1965), passed by Congress and signed by then-President Lyndon B. Johnson.

Advocacy can take place in two forms. The first form of advocacy is through our most basic right—the right to vote. This vote can take place one of two ways, either through voting for a person or voting for policy in the form of ballot initiatives. The second form of advocacy is through the influence of policies that elected officials either support or oppose.

The first form of advocacy, voting, is the most basic right given to all citizens of this great nation. For the life of me I don't know why people choose not to utilize this most cherished right as American citizens. People simply don't vote at the rate that they ought to vote. There are also too many within the electorate that simply don't vote in an informed manner. Too large a number of voters don't do their due diligence on the candidates on the ballot. They don't research their policies, their promises, or their stances on issues affecting our day-to-day lives. By becoming informed on the candidate and his or her policy positions, you are setting yourself up to be an informed citizen that can make decisions in the best interest of our cities, our counties, our states, and our nation. It is essential that you look at what the elected official or candidate says, does, and believes. You must see if what the elected official or candidate says, does, and believes is in alignment with what you as a citizen believe. We must vote along the line that mostly resembles our ideology. We must vote based on our faith in the people offering themselves for public service as well as the policies that they claim to believe and espouse. Therefore, we must vote based upon people and policy. It is okay to vote on both the character of the person and their ideology, their belief system. We must vote for people who espouse the positions that we believe most closely align with our own set of beliefs.

The second form of advocacy is accomplished by communicating one's support or opposition to a policy or policies with elected officials. Advocacy is pushing for views and policies that are aligned with your belief system. Democracy is a government by the people; it is the rule of the majority. It's a government in which supreme power is vested in the people. It is a representative form of government that involves periodically held free elections.

This means that our government, by sheer reality of its makeup, can and should be influenced by those who make up the government: the *people*. It is the duty of the people of these United States to steer the direction of this nation, whether through policy or through its elected officials.

The nation is like a cruise line, a ship. The rudder of this ship is the taxpaying citizens of the United States of America. The act of the rudder moving to the right or to the left is the advocacy of its citizens that steers the ship of this nation in the direction it should go. In theory, this is how the nation should work. However, we know that it is big business and special interest organizations that many times steer the ship of this nation. This nation can be likened to the song penned by the infamous rap group, the Wu-Tang Clan, "C.R.E.A.M. (Cash Rules Everything Around Me)." This song is indicative of how the political infrastructure of this nation operates both in campaigns and in actual governance. It is for this reason that individuals and organizations that truly represent the will of the people must step forward to dictate the direction of this nation.

Individuals and organizations alike can steer the direction of this nation through advocacy. Persons and groups can make their voices heard by advocating their positions with elected officials who have authority over a whole litany of issues. Following are some helpful tips for political advocacy activities you may undertake.

Quick Foundational Tips for Advocacy:

1. Define the issue.
2. Create list of all elected officials.
3. Find contact information for elected officials—websites, mailing addresses, email addresses, phone numbers, fax numbers.
4. Research each elected official's job duties and responsibilities.
5. Research issues based upon each level of government's responsibility.

6. Determine what level of government and/or elected official has responsibility over your issue or concern.
7. Investigate meeting dates and agendas.
8. Follow voting records and patterns.
9. Share your position with your elected officials via email, fax, or mail and make known your position to the elected official and/or the designated representative in letter format.
10. Share your position with family, friends, neighbors, church members, associates, etc. and ask them to share with the appropriated elected officials—give them all the contact information to correspond with their elected officials.

I have a saying: Those who are reactive will always serve those who are proactive. People who are reactive tend to let things happen in their life. Proactive people tend to make things happen in their life. Reactive people generally go with the flow; they follow the winds of life, whereas proactive people tend to go against the winds of life if they are against the plans they have for their life. Those who are reactive generally are not very opinionated, whereas proactive people generally have very distinct opinions by which they operate their lives.

The act of advocacy can only been done effectively by persons who are considerably proactive in their approach to politics. The very definition of advocacy lends itself only to a proactive approach. Unfortunately, the majority of Americans are very reactive in their politics. The majority of Americans are incredibly apathetic concerning politics. This apathy is shown in two forms. One is by not participating in the political process (not voting). The second is by participating strictly according to some divisive reasons i.e. partisan, economic, or even racial politics. A telltale sign of apathy in the political process is when a voter votes solely along party lines. If you are a Democrat and you only vote for Democrats, or a Republican only for Republicans, you are apathetic towards the political process. This is a very reactionary way of participating in the political process. When you vote in this manner, you are simply like sheep being led either to safety or to the slaughter. In this manner you are entrusting your direction solely based on the leader's discretion. As a voter operating in this manner, you provide no critical thought to the issue or the subject matter at hand. In this manner you never allow your core values to lead you through the political process. You are simply relying on the core values of others to lead you. Nehemiah, in the book that shares his name in the Bible, is an example of a proactive figure. Nehemiah's example is one that has him responding to a situation in a very proactive way that completely changed the situation for the good of others. Nehemiah lived in the fifth century BC. The story of Nehemiah in the Bible begins with him receiving news that the home he once knew, Jerusalem, was in great distress. He learned that his country was unprotected and its walls were in ruins. The walls of Jerusalem symbolized the strength of Jerusalem. The walls were the key to protecting the city. After Jerusalem was held captive and a majority of its citizens were exiled to foreign lands, the nation itself was left desolate and vulnerable. Upon hearing the news, Nehemiah took it upon himself to rebuild the nation's walls. Nehemiah saw that there was a need, and he proactively moved to make a difference in the lives of the people. Nehemiah, in effect, lobbied on behalf of the general welfare of the city of Jerusalem. He saw a real need, and he worked to address the needs of the city. Nehemiah operated in similar fashion to the wisdom given to King Lemuel by his mother in Proverbs 31:8–9 when she says to "open your mouth for the speechless" and to "plead the cause of the poor and needy." During this time, both the city and the people of Jerusalem were in a very vulnerable state. The walls of Jerusalem lay in ruin, exposing them to attack on every side. As a result, both the city and the people themselves were in need of someone to come to their rescue. Nehemiah was that person. Nehemiah was an advocate, and because of his advocacy, the walls of Jerusalem were rebuilt in record time. Let's take the aforementioned tips for advocacy and see how they align with Nehemiah's story.

✪ **Define the issue.**

Nehemiah 1:3: "And they said to me, 'The survivors who are left from the captivity in the province are there in great distress and reproach. The wall of Jerusalem is also broken down, and its gates are burned with fire.'"

Commentary: The wall of Jerusalem is in shambles.

✪ **Create list of all elected officials.**

Nehemiah 2:1: "And it came to pass in the month of Nisan, in the twentieth year of King Artaxerxes, when wine was before him, that I took the wine and gave it to the king."

Commentary: King Artaxerxes is the ruler of the day and the person in charge.

✪ **Find contact information for elected officials.**

Nehemiah 1:1: "The words of Nehemiah the son of Hachaliah. It came to pass in the month of Chislev, in the twentieth year, as I was in Shushan the citadel."

Nehemiah 2:1: "And it came to pass in the month of Nisan, in the twentieth year of King Artaxerxes, when wine was before him, that I took the wine and gave it to the king."

Commentary: Nehemiah was in Shushan (Capitol of Persia), and the next text says that he gave wine to King Artaxerxes, which suggests that the King was located in Shushan.

✪ **Research elected official job duties and responsibilities.**

Commentary: The King ruled over Persia, but also over the people of Jerusalem in captivity.

✪ **Research issues based upon each level of government's responsibility.**

Nehemiah 2:7: "Furthermore I said to the king, 'If it pleases the king, let letters be given to me for the governors of the region beyond the River, that they must permit me to pass through till I come to Judah.'"

Commentary: The king also had influence and power over the governors of the region, which allowed Nehemiah safe travel to Jerusalem.

✪ **Determine what level of government and/or elected official has responsibility over your issue or concern.**
[See previous Scripture, Nehemiah 2:7]

Commentary: The King approved of Nehemiah going home to rebuild the walls.

✪ **Investigate meeting dates and agendas.**
[Scripture Reference Not Applicable]

Commentary: There isn't anything in the text that is applicable, but remember that in Nehemiah 2:1, Nehemiah brought wine to the King, so it is safe to say that he knew where the King would be and when he would be there.

✪ **Follow voting record and patterns.**
[Scripture Reference Not Applicable]

No Commentary: There were no votes made, just a singular decision to be made by the King.

✪ **Share your position with your elected officials.**

Nehemiah 2:4–5: "Then the king said to me, 'What do you request?' So I prayed to the God of heaven. And I said to the king, 'If it pleases the king, and if your servant has found favor in your sight, I ask that you send me to Judah, to the city of my fathers' tombs, that I may rebuild it.'"

Commentary: Nehemiah asked the King for his request to be honored and the King obliged his request to travel to Jerusalem in order to rebuild the walls. This request was made verbally.

⊙ **Share your position with family, friends, neighbors, church members, associates, and so on and ask them to join the fight.**

Nehemiah 2:17–18: "Then I said to them, 'You see the distress that we are in, how Jerusalem lies waste, and its gates are burned with fire. Come and let us build the wall of Jerusalem, that we may no longer be a reproach.' And I told them of the hand of my God which had been good upon me, and also of the king's words that he had spoken to me. So they said, 'Let us rise up and build.' Then they set their hands to this good work."

Commentary: Nehemiah shared the issue with others and asked them to join in his quest to rebuild the walls. They joined him and began to rebuild the walls together.

The record also shows that Nehemiah worked to facilitate change in the corruption and evils that were going on in Jerusalem. He worked as a type of governor in the temple (Nehemiah 10:1). He commanded many things in the land and he made many appointments to oversee various areas of responsibility.

Nehemiah, in effect, was the leader of the city of Jerusalem. Upon completion of the wall, he began to put people in charge of the city. He elected to place Hanani and Hannaniah (Nehemiah 7:2) in positions of power. He established a genealogy of all the people (Nehemiah 7:5). He appointed treasurers over the storehouse (Nehemiah 13:13). Nehemiah, essentially, was a type of savior for the city of Jerusalem and a real leader.

Nehemiah was not only concerned about the city of Jerusalem, but also for the people of Jerusalem. When he learned that the Levites were not being compensated for their work in the temple, he set them in their place (Nehemiah 13:10–11). When he learned that people were not following the laws of God concerning the Sabbath, he got the people in order (Nehemiah 13:19). Nehemiah worked as an advocate on behalf of the city, which equipped and prepared him to lead the city. He was qualified to be in a seat of authority when he rebuilt the walls. His leadership led to the revitalization of that nation. Nehemiah is a leader that elected leaders ought to emulate. Nehemiah is the type of leader that voters ought to elect throughout this nation.

Some may ask—how will we know what type of person we ought to elect to lead us? How do we establish a process to filter candidates so that we may select the best person for the job? We can take the example of Nehemiah as our guide. Nehemiah was a visionary. He saw a need concerning his community—the walls were in desolation (Nehemiah 1:3). Nehemiah had compassion for his people—he had a heart for the city of Jerusalem and its people. Nehemiah was sympathetic for the plight of his people—he wept when he heard the news about the condition of the city (Nehemiah 1:4). The record shows that he began to pray on behalf of the city and its people (Nehemiah 1:5). He repented on behalf of the past sins of the people and asked for forgiveness and help on their behalf. Then Nehemiah put his faith into action. Remember the Scripture, "Faith without works is dead"? His faith pushed him to work on behalf of the city. He asked the King of Persia, under whose rulership he had lived, to allow him to go to Jerusalem and to rebuild it (Nehemiah 2:5).

Characteristics of Nehemiah:

- ✪ Compassionate
- ✪ Sympathetic
- ✪ Prayerful
- ✪ Sensitive
- ✪ Proactive
- ✪ Insightful

Nehemiah was an advocate for his city and his people well before he operated in a role of leadership within the city. Actually, his advocacy on behalf of the city was leadership in itself. In this same manner, we must look at the history and background of a candidate seeking office. You want to see whether the candidate's background is relevant to the work he or she is seeking to do as an elected official. This is a good indicator as to how that person will operate in the future as an elected official.

Civic Process

There are three important aspects of the civic process—voter registration, voter education, and voter mobilization. The first, voter registration, is the very first action for engaging the political system. This simply consists of registering citizens to vote. In order to vote, you must be registered; that's a no-brainer. The second, voter education, is a little more difficult. The first, voter registration, is simply filling out a sheet of paper—name, address, age, and other basic relevant demographic information. You are simply reacting to questions posed to you on paper. The second, voter education, causes you to proactively learn the lay of the political land. It causes you to learn and understand each level of government's roles and responsibilities. It sets you up to be interactive and responsive to the actions of the government. It allows you to truly engage the government concerning its policies and practices. The third, voter mobilization, is when you use your status as a registered voter and utilize your education as a voter to truly effect change in our government. The lowest form of mobilization is voting. A higher form of mobilization is when voters takes their status as registered voters and use their acquired education to tell the government, via elected officials, what they should or shouldn't be doing. Voter mobilization is when voters get a chance to make their voices heard through letters, emails, phone calls, and so on regarding their belief in government. Advocacy is a type of voter mobilization.

Dr. Martin Luther King, Jr. says concerning the civic process in his speech, "Where Do We Go From Here: Chaos or Community?": "And so we shall have to do more than register and more than vote; we shall have to create leaders who embody virtues we can respect, who have moral and ethical principles we can applaud with enthusiasm."

Dr. King is speaking of doing more than just registering to vote and casting your individual ballot. Part of the civic process is also creating the kind of government you want to see. As a democracy, we can endorse and support the type and quality of public servants we desire to see. This is a higher level of civic participation. However, in order to "create leaders," as Dr. King suggests, we must understand what we stand for. We must know what we believe and be able to effectively communicate it.

This higher level of civic participation will raise the level of the individual's focus. No longer will the individual focus solely on his or her one vote. An enlightened voter will transcend beyond his or her own personal situation within the political process. The enlightened voter will work to make our nation a better place. He or she will do this by insuring that both our laws and lawmakers are suitable for governing this nation. The enlightened voter will be an advocate for that which he or she believes in, whether through the support of people or through the policies within the framework of our great democracy.

PROGRESSION OF POLICY

DEMOCRACY

↓

BELIEFS

Driven by:
Family Values, Faith in God, Understanding Scripture

↓

IDEOLOGY

↓

POLICY

↓

POLITICS
(Chapter Focus: Politics 101)

selves over the next four, eight, even twenty years. It spoke to the policy direction of this nation. It spoke to the future of the nation's international reputation. There would never have been a President Barack Obama had it not been for the support and investments of everyday people who cared about the leadership and the future of this nation. There would not have been certain policies advanced concerning health care, foreign policy, climate change, the economy, the Middle East, and others had it not been for President Obama, a Democrat, being in office. Conversely, the policies that were espoused over the previous presidency would not have been advanced if President Bush had not been in office.

As previously stated, when I was approached by my friend, Erik Burton, about running for the county commission, I had no real understanding about what a commissioner did. As active as I was in political life, I lacked an understanding of how local government and politics operated. As much as I called myself an active and well-versed participant in the political world, there was one weakness in my understanding of politics, which concerned local government. I soon found out how local government was the linchpin to the basic quality of our lives.

Tip O'Neill coined the phrase "All politics is local." This basic statement points to the fact that at any level of government, the heart of any matter is connected to how it affects the daily lives of one's constituents. To hold an elected office at the local level means that one must deal with the day-to-day lives and issues of everyday citizens. Any city or county government is considered local government. It's where the rubber meets the road; it's where basic quality of life issues are resolved. Locally elected officials (no disrespect to other elected officials) are the officials that most directly affect people's day-to-day lives. County commissions deal with issues that most people take for granted. Local issues typically are not the issues that are sensationalized in the media and given much attention by the citizenry. For example, county commissioners are rarely asked about their thoughts on potholes or what they think about water or sewer systems. They are not asked about their thoughts on county parks. They are not asked about the need for a police or a fire department. They are not asked about the county dump truck or the landfill the county owns. However, these are areas that taxpaying citizens deal with most frequently on a day-to-day and almost a minute-by-minute basis. These issues are taken for granted until something goes wrong with them. You don't think about clear and clean water until it turns brown. You don't think about the basic maintenance of roads until there is a big pothole on your street. You don't think about the police department unless there is break-in at your house and the police don't arrive to your house for an hour after your call.

Most people don't realize that the elected officials that most help to determine the quality of your community are the locally elected officials. It is the local elected officials who help to make your community clean through its sanitation department. They help to keep your community safe through its police department. They help to keep your community healthy through its board of health. They help to keep the quality of new buildings and development nice through its planning department. They help to keep quality jobs in your community through its economic development department. However, most people don't know this reality because they don't know what their local elected officials do and how they affect their lives.

It is important to note that potholes, parks, water, trash, police, and fire don't have a party affiliation. There is not a Democratic pothole and a Republican park. Most of what local elected officials do is nonpartisan and people like it that way. This may seem like a Civic 101 lesson, but it is critical for the betterment of government. Local government is generally about access to resources, not partisan politics; it is about communities and neighborhoods getting connected with the supply of local government's assets.

When I campaigned for my first elected office, I told potential supporters and supporters alike that I needed them to be engaged in their local government. I told them I desperately needed them to hold my feet to the fire. I needed them to be well versed on the roles and responsibilities of a county commissioner. I needed them to hold me accountable for the decisions and votes I would make as a commissioner. I needed them, through their personal commitment to our county, to make me a better elected official.

Local elected officials ought to represent the interest of the people. They ought to reflect the desires and wishes of the people. I believe elected officials are only as good as the electorate mandates them to be. I believe the elected officials will be only as good as they are held accountable to be and every voter should know that they are empowered to hold their representatives accountable. This begins with having a healthy understanding of the government and its authority.

There are various levels of government that have specific roles and responsibilities throughout the nation. They all affect our lives in different ways. The local, state, and federal levels of government all have varying levels of roles and responsibilities in our lives.

Local government consists of the following:

✪ Municipal/City Government

- Elected Officials: Mayors, City Councils

✪ County/Parish Government

- Elected Officials: County Chairs, County Executives, County Commissioners, District Attorney, Sheriff, Solicitor General, Tax Commissioner

✪ Local School Systems (City or County)

- School Board President, School Board Members

✪ Local Courts

State government consists of the following:

✪ Governor, Lt. Governor, Secretary of State, Attorney General, Labor Commissioner, Insurance Commissioner, Agriculture Commissioner, School Superintendent, State Representatives, State Senators, State Court Judge, Superior Court Judge, State Supreme Courts (some appointed, some elected), etc.

Federal government consists of the following:

✪ President, Vice President, United State Congress (House of Representatives, Senate), etc.

- Important Figures (not elected, appointed and confirmed by POTUS and Congress): U.S. Supreme Court, Cabinet Members—Attorney General, Secretary's of the following: State, Defense, Education, Labor, etc.

  ★ This list is not an exhaustive one and may have unintentionally omitted certain positions

Politics are all about access to and control of resources. These resources are revenues realized from the taxation of income, property, and consumption and from various fees and fines. Taxes are the primary way revenue is realized at any level of government. Each level of government will decide for themselves the degree of taxation on its citizens. The revenue realized from taxation is then utilized to cover the basic cost of operating government. Taxpayers simply desire for government to operate effectively. They desire for services to be offered efficiently with as low a tax burden as possible. People elect people to positions of authority because they expect them to effectively govern the administration of government. They expect elected officials to run government in a manner that respects each dollar contributed for the administration of government.

In my role as a county commissioner and in any role thereafter, I have to make critical budget decisions concerning resources and services. Let's look at a hypothetical situation that reflects the basic issues of government on every level.

Hypothetical County Budget:

⮑ County Budget = $1 Billion (Revenues generated from taxes, fines and fees)

⮑ County Services (Expenditures) = police, fire, parks and recreation, water and sewer systems, roads and drainage, and economic development, sheriff's office, district attorney's office, solicitor general's office, county clerk's office, and various levels of judges

A $1 billion budget may sound like a lot, but if you have a million people in your county, then it becomes tough to decide how to distribute these dollars across all of these areas. The Bible says, "For where your treasure is, there your heart will be also." (Luke 12:34). This means that the way you spend your money represents what you hold most important. The way you spend your money says what you hold as priority. For example, many elected officials at the local level proclaim public safety as their number one priority. However, if it is not reflected within the allocation of resources, then that proclamation is simply an empty promise. Likewise, many candidates for office declare education as their number-one issue, but when elected they steer clear of true reform in our educational system.

The vision of the elected official is critical for the operation of government. It is critical that the elected official's vision, to some degree, follow the will and desires of the taxpaying citizen. The reality of most governments is that there are always more needs than there are resources. The access to and control of resources are critical components to any government. An elected official must determine what the priorities of the people are and they must fight for the allocation of resources accordingly. The people should dictate to elected officials the priorities of resources, not the other way around.

On a different level, the federal government has many competing factions for its resources. As I pen this book, the United States Congress has recently deliberated over an unprecedented move to reform our health care system. This is more than a simple partisan move. It's about the estimated fifty million uninsured people in this nation who need help. However, this won't occur within a vacuum. This is nearly a *trillion*-dollar endeavor. The most recent votes in Congress on this legislation have proven to be very partisan. Those voting for the legislation, although not perfect, cited the need for something better than the status quo, something that serves to cover the uninsured, if not at minimum reducing the number of uninsured throughout the nation. Those voting against the measure cited typically one of two reasons. The first reason was that they fundamentally didn't believe that this country ought to foot the bill for such a large endeavor. The second was not because they disagreed with the need for reform, but because they disagreed with the proposed measures of reform. With almost a trillion dollars on the line, the fight for the control of resources was priority number one. The major question to be answered is—where do we get the money to cover such a monumental task? Although the running joke regarding the federal government is that when we need money we just print more currency, it's not really how government works. Our options are pretty simple: (1) we can increase taxes to pay for it, (2) we can cut spending in other areas, (3) we can borrow money to cover the cost, or (4) some combination of the aforementioned options.

For all of the policy stances our elected officials may have, none of this means a hill of beans if there is not the appropriate level of resources appropriated to cover their subsequent costs. There must be a corresponding fiscal commitment connected to any policy decision in order to make it a reality. Thus, the real end game of politics is the control of resources. It is the control of resources that wields the real power to facilitate change in politics.

When deciding whom you will vote for on Election Day,

ask yourself the question—who would you most trust with your money? Who would you feel most comfortable giving the responsibility of managing your hard-earned tax dollars? Who would you most trust with the trillions of dollars of taxpayers' hard-earned money to lead this nation? Obviously you would want someone controlling the nation's resources with which you share common beliefs and values. You would want someone you could trust with that responsibility. I am sure you would want someone in office that would be a good steward in the allocation and distribution of the nation's resources. That's why it is a critical exercise to formulate and know your ideology. By making this determination, you will be well positioned to communicate your beliefs to those who are responsible for the distribution of resources, whether through appointed or elected office.

PROGRESSION OF POLICY

DEMOCRACY

◑

BELIEFS

Driven by:
Family Values, Faith in God, Understanding Scripture

◑

IDEOLOGY

◑

POLICY

◑

POLITICS
(Chapter focus: My God, My Politics)

CHAPTER ELEVEN

My God, My Politics

Pure and undefiled religion before God and the Father is this: to visit orphans and widows in their trouble, and to keep oneself unspotted from the world.

—James 1:27

M y *God, My Politics* is an opportunity for everyday people to develop their own belief system, one that is developed from an internal perspective, one informed by their faith perspective. This may sound like a broken record, but your belief in God should have an influence on your politics. The Scripture above is an example of how your politics can be influenced by your faith. It also stands as an example of my politics being influenced by my faith. The Scripture speaks about helping those most in need, helping those who would be considered the least of these. Orphans and widows during that period of time were considered the most vulnerable. Whenever there is a reference to an orphan or to a widow, one should clearly note that it is referencing someone in need. Thus, we clearly know that, as members of the human race, we are to help the orphan, the widow, and most importantly, those in real need. Today we can infer that also those who are physically or mentally challenged, drug-addicted, homeless, unemployed, poor, and uninsured, just to name a few, are the those who we are to care for and look after; this, as the Scripture says, is "pure and undefiled religion."

However, assisting those in need looks different to different people and to different political parties. I think it's safe to say that the majority of Americans believe just as the Scripture says—that as humans we are to help those most in need. I also believe that most Americans believe that government, to some degree, ought to have a hand in helping those persons in our society. This can be summed up by the verse of Scripture that says, "Love God and love thy neighbor" (Luke 10:27). The point of departure from a political perspective comes with the question—how much should we help those who are in need? Additionally, who exactly ought to be helped when they are in need? For example, there are those in our society that are in real need of assistance through no fault of their own. An orphan clearly did not have a say as to whether he or she would eventually become an orphan. However, people that use illicit and illegal drugs have at some point (especially prior to any addiction) made the choice for themselves that they would live this type of lifestyle. The point of debate then remains whether you only help the one, because he or she had no choice in the matter, or whether you help everyone in need, regardless of the reason for their plight.

This may sound a bit flippant, but money does not grow on trees! We have a limited amount of resources to cover an ever-growing expanse of issues. What we do with these resources is very important. So the question of who receives help vacillates back and forth from a social responsibility conversation to a budgetary one. In the budgetary scenario, the person is no longer the central focus of the conversation but is relegated to the periphery of the debate. Some elected officials may say that the most important part of their job is to protect the official interests of the nation itself. By focusing on budgetary issues first, they are protecting the strength of the nation as a corporate body. Whereas, others may say that the most important aspect of their responsibilities is for the interests of the people themselves, by whom they were elected and whom they serve. These are two different perspectives regarding governance. However, they need not be mutually exclusive. The former will ask how this affects the state, and the latter will ask how this affects the people. Each perspective will lead the elected official down a different road of governance. There is, however, also a possibility that both perspectives can lead to the same place. This can only take place when there is a balanced approach to the distribution of resources in this nation.

A balanced approach is when the heart of the government and its elected representatives is directed toward helping the people it represents. However, we must be prudent in the distribution of this nation's resources. We can't simply dole out resources for everyone and for every issue someone may have. There must be standards in place, monetary limits on assistance, strict evaluations performed, and strict records maintained in order to carefully monitor the amount of assistance given for any program offered. Neither the social responsibility nor the budgetary perspective is right or wrong. Balance is the key word regarding one's approach to governing. Elected officials must be concerned for both the people they represent and the political jurisdiction they represent.

For example, the economic recession that this nation is experiencing as I write this book is affecting the real lives of people in our nation. The economy has tanked over the past few years; homes have been foreclosed in record numbers, jobs have been lost by the hundreds of thousands each month, and the stock market has experienced lows like never experienced in recent history. Efforts such as the America Recovery and Re-Investment Act (ARRA) legislation were intended to stem the tragic consequences of this poor economy on both people and governments at every level. Their intent was to put people back to work, as well as to assist local and state governments do their jobs as they have experienced major revenue shortfalls. The reality of health care reform, as was presented in Congress, was meant to address the rising health care cost and to reduce the number of uninsured throughout the country. In both examples, efforts were made to affect both the lives of citizens and to stabilize government.

It is critical to have citizens who are healthy, wealthy, and contributing members of society. It is important to the vitality of this nation. The better the state of our citizenry, the better the state of our nation! When we have healthier citizens we have less pressure on our health care system. When we have more literate citizens, there is less pressure on our welfare system. When we have gainfully employed citizens, there is less pressure on our criminal justice systems. Healthy, wealthy, educated members of our society make for a healthier and wealthier nation. Therefore, one cannot lose sight of one perspective over the other. One cannot choose to focus solely on social policy while simultaneously forgetting about the financial implications it may have on our nation's finances. It's a balance that each elected official must deliberate over each and every day that they serve.

There must also be a balanced approached to governing when incorporating faith in the realm of politics. Many have used the extremes of both faith and politics to keep the two apart. However, real value is added when there is a balanced approach and understanding of both. The following are examples of these extremes:

Faith:

- Wholly sacred
- Heavenly minded only
- Focus on God only
- Focus inside church
- Looks only above
- Overly spiritual

Politics:

- ➲ Wholly secular
- ➲ Earthly minded only
- ➲ Focus on humanity only
- ➲ Focus outside church
- ➲ Look only within
- ➲ Overly humanist

The extremes of faith and of politics serve to keep one from ever engaging the other. The extremity of faith looks upward and the extremity of politics looks inward. Faith looking upward looks to God only for its help. Politics looking inward looks within only for its help. Faith looks only toward God for its solutions, whereas politics looks inward to humanity for the resolution of its problems and for the advancement of society. The problem with these extremes is that they leave an imbalance. Faith tells politics that politics has nothing to offer faith. Conversely, politics tells faith that faith has nothing to offer politics. These extremities leave a void within the earth that also leaves humanity lacking.

However, the Apostle Paul, in his letter to the Philippians in the New Testament, gives what could be seen as a better approach to life. As highlighted above, these extremes can be characterized by living in the present or living in the hereafter. Paul gives us his thoughts concerning the two:

> *For to me, to live is Christ, and to die is gain. But if I live on in the flesh, this will mean fruit from my labor; yet what I shall choose I cannot tell. For I am hard-pressed between the two, having a desire to depart and be with Christ, which is far better. Nevertheless to remain in the flesh is more needful for you. And being confident of this, I know that I shall remain and continue with you all for your progress and joy of faith, that your rejoicing for me may be more abundant in Jesus Christ by my coming to you again. (Philippians 1:21–26)*

Paul is saying that, as Christians, our ultimate resting place is with Christ. Although Paul acknowledges that his ultimate desire was to be with Christ, he also realized that there was much left to do here on earth. Therefore, although heaven is our ultimate goal, there is something great that must be done in and through our lives while here on earth. Paul acknowledges that although it would be great to personally be with Christ, it would be better if he were to remain on earth for the benefit of the people he served. Paul understood that although his personal relationship with God was very important, his relationship with the people of Phillipi was also important. He realized that his personal relationship with God was only part of what God desired for his life. Paul understood that God desired his relationship with him to be connected with his relationship with humanity. Paul knew that God desired him to be a servant to others. Paul lived by the commandment that urges us to love God and to love thy neighbor. Christians who focus only on their personal piety and their personal relationship with God to the absence of their relationship with people have simply misunderstood God's desires. We must understand that there is a duality to life as commanded to us by Jesus.

This duality is the love of God and also the love of humanity. This proposition is a true cause-and-effect type of relationship. Loving God causes you to love your neighbor. Conversely, when you truly love your neighbor, who is God's creation, you can't help but to love God. I submit that one cannot faithfully love God if he or she does not faithfully love their neighbor. It is this type of love that God desires for us to act out. John 3:16 says, "For God so loved the world that He gave His only begotten Son, that whoever believes in Him should not perish but have everlasting life." God loved us so much that He gave His son for our sake. Love is an action. God desires us to love one another through action. One cannot truly love their neighbor if they do not have a genuine and pure love for God, the kind of love displayed in 1 Corinthians 13:

Though I speak with the tongues of men and of angels, but have not love, I have become sounding brass or a clanging cymbal. And though I have the gift of prophecy, and understand all mysteries and all knowledge, and though I have all faith, so that I could remove mountains, but have not love, I am nothing. And though I bestow all my goods to feed the poor, and though I give my body to be burned, but have not love, it profits me nothing. Love suffers long and is kind; love does not envy; love does not parade itself, is not puffed up; does not behave rudely, does not seek its own, is not provoked, thinks no evil; does not rejoice in iniquity, but rejoices in the truth; bears all things, believes all things, hopes all things, endures all things. Love never fails. But whether there are prophecies, they will fail; whether there are tongues, they will cease; whether there is knowledge, it will vanish away. For we know in part and we prophesy in part. But when that which is perfect has come, then that which is in part will be done away. When I was a child, I spoke as a child, I understood as a child, I thought as a child; but when I became a man, I put away childish things. For now we see in a mirror, dimly, but then face to face. Now I know in part, but then I shall know just as I also am known. And now abide faith, hope, love, these three; but the greatest of these is love. (1 Corinthians 13)

This type of love, as shown in 1 Corinthians 13, is one that is unconditional. It is the type of love that God shows towards humanity each and every day. It is this love that allows us to truly take the focus off of ourselves and place it on loving our neighbor. It is this love that empowers us to love sacrificially. It is this love that creates the "beloved community," as was referenced on many occasions by Rev. Martin Luther King, Jr. This community is one that promotes love instead of hate; it embraces love instead of prejudice; it turns toward love instead of war.

I overheard Reverend Jesse Jackson say that "too many people in the church worship only to worship." He went on to say that this is the wrong mindset to have in worship. What he meant was that we ought to "worship to serve." This statement falls in line with the Two Great Commands—to love God first, and then to love thy neighbor. The act of worship says to God that you love Him. The act of serving shows that you love God. Jesus, after asking Peter (his disciple) three times if he loved him, stated, "If you love me, feed my sheep" (John 21:15–17). God said if you love Him, then you will love His people through service. One cannot claim to love God and refuse to help that which God loves the most, His people. That is why the story of the Good Samaritan holds such a powerful lesson.

The story of the Good Samaritan in Luke 10:30–37 talks about a certain man who was on a journey and was attacked by a band of robbers. The robbers stripped the gentleman of his clothing, wounded him, and departed, leaving him half dead. After being attacked, a Priest and a Levite both saw the injured man and passed on the other side of the street so as to not engage the victim. However, a Samaritan came to him and helped nurse him back to health. He bandaged his wounds and he paid for his stay at the local hotel.

Then Jesus answered and said: "A certain man went down from Jerusalem to Jericho, and fell among thieves, who stripped him of his clothing, wounded him, and departed, leaving him half dead. Now by chance a certain priest came down that road. And when he saw him, he passed by on the other side. Likewise a Levite, when he arrived at the place, came and looked, and passed by on the other side. But a certain Samaritan, as he journeyed, came where he was. And when he saw him, he had compassion. So he went to him and bandaged his wounds, pouring on oil and wine; and he set him on his own animal, brought him to an inn, and took care of him. On the next day, when he departed, he took out two denarii, gave them to the innkeeper, and said to him, 'Take care of him; and whatever more you spend, when I come again, I will repay you.' So which of these three do you think was neighbor to him who fell among the thieves?" And he said, "He who showed mercy on him." Then Jesus said to him, "Go and do likewise." (Luke 10:30–37)

Jesus told this parable as a response to a lawyer that asked him how he could inherit eternal life. The lawyer quickly pointed to the Law of Moses, which said to love God and love thy neighbor. A couple of observations concerning this parable: Observation #1: This parable taught the hearer of the parable, the lawyer, the difference between the letter and the spirit of the law. The letter simply recounts what the law says, to love God and love neighbor. The spirit actually puts the law into action. Observation #2: This parable taught us to love even our enemies. The Samaritans and the Jews were essentially enemies, and thus it is more than ironic that both a Priest and a Levite passed the Jewish man in need. It was a perceived enemy who came to the aid of the man in need. The Good Samaritan can be interpreted as being the image of a good man. A good man follows not only the letter of the law but also the spirit of the law. The good man not only helps those who are considered friends, but also helps those who may be different in background, experience, and even race. As a closing statement, Jesus told the onlookers to go and do likewise. I am of the mindset that this story has both life and political ramifications. We are to give assistance to those who are in need. We are to give of our resources to those in need even when it is inconvenient. Let me apologize in advance for reading too much into this Scripture, but the Priest and the Levite could have very well been too busy, too caught up in their own responsibilities to help the man in need. Thus, the Samaritan provides a good example of helping someone even when it's inconvenient and even when it's seemingly unpopular.

Jesus gives another parable that highlights the importance of helping others. This parable is concerning the judgment of the nations. In Matthew 25:34–46, Jesus tells the story of a king talking to his people. It speaks about people inheriting the kingdom as a result of their deeds. He says that the people who took care of those most in need (those hungry, thirsty, naked, and sick) were the ones who inherited the kingdom. Conversely, those who decided not to help those in need would receive "everlasting punishment.

> *"Then the King will say to those on His right hand, "Come, you blessed of My Father, inherit the kingdom prepared for you from the foundation of the world: for I was hungry and you gave Me food; I was thirsty and you gave Me drink; I was a stranger and you took Me in; I was naked and you clothed Me; I was sick and you visited Me; I was in prison and you came to Me." Then the righteous will answer Him, saying, "Lord, when did we see You hungry and feed You, or thirsty and give You drink? When did we see You a stranger and take You in, or naked and clothe You? Or when did we see You sick, or in prison, and come to You?" And the King will answer and say to them, "Assuredly, I say to you, inasmuch as you did it to one of the least of these My brethren, you did it to Me." Then He will also say to those on the left hand, "Depart from Me, you cursed, into the everlasting fire prepared for the devil and his angels: for I was hungry and you gave Me no food; I was thirsty and you gave Me no drink; I was a stranger and you did not take Me in, naked and you did not clothe Me, sick and in prison and you did not visit Me." Then they also will answer Him, saying, "Lord, when did we see You hungry or thirsty or a stranger or naked or sick or in prison, and did not minister to You?" Then He will answer them, saying, "Assuredly, I say to you, inasmuch as you did not do it to one of the least of these, you did not do it to Me." And these will go away into everlasting punishment, but the righteous into eternal life. (Matthew 25:34–46)*

The type and content of your faith will have a direct influence over your politics. It is safe to say that your politics will follow your faith. Jim Wallis, an evangelical Christian writer and political activist, best known as the founder and editor of *Sojourner's*

Magazine and author of *God's Politics*, says, "The best response to bad religion is better religion, not secularism." Thus, your politics is determined in great part by the nature and substance of your faith or belief system.

Our faith has tremendous power to influence both our policy and politics. However, it is the choice of every person to allow their core beliefs to affect the outcomes of their lives. God has never forced anyone to do anything. God is a God of choice. We have the choice to do good or to do evil. We have the choice to embrace the Christian message or to reject it. Each decision that is made has underlying consequences.

Deuteronomy 30:19 says, "I call heaven and earth as witnesses today against you, that I have set before you life and death, blessing and cursing; therefore choose life, that both you and your descendants may live."

This means that the decisions that are made in life have consequences. Those consequences, as given in this Scripture, are life or death, blessings or curses. Choices that are made in life have consequences. Likewise, policy choices made in the political world have far-reaching consequences. As elected officials or even laypersons, one cannot simply allow others to determine what policies or politics one promotes or supports. If our democracy is to truly live out its creed, we need every citizen to develop his or her own personal policy stances.

The question, therefore, must be answered—what does my faith say about the areas concerning public policy? Following are various policy areas for you to consider regarding your own belief system.

★Policy Areas:

Role of Government	Health Care
Criminal Justice	Foreign Policy
Fiscal Policy	Education

Military Defense   Environment
Social Welfare   Social Security
Transportation   Tax Policy
Economy   Etc.

* This, by no means, is an exhaustive list.

Although the Bible rarely speaks directly concerning many of these topics, there are real clues in Scripture that can help one form a reasonably informed opinion. Through the process of exegesis, we can ascertain the original intent of the writings. Through the process of exposition, we can then overlay the original meaning of the Scripture to form an opinion relevant to our current experience.

Role of Government

Since the inception of this nation there has been a debate about the role of government in the lives of the American people. Should government be intricately involved in the life of its citizens or have a very limited role? This is a major question, the answer to which will dictate just about every other opinion concerning issues of public policy. Some believe that government should get involved in only those activities that citizens simply cannot provide for themselves—such as public works projects (roads and sewer) or defense projects (Army, Navy, Marines, Air Force). Others believe that government should also get involved in those activities that would support the greater good and welfare of society, such as public education and various levels of public assistance. Your answer to the role of government in the life of its citizens will determine the position you will likely take on a whole host of political and policy issues. As opinions go within political parties, Republicans generally believe in a very limited role of government in the lives of people, typically focusing heavily on defense and capitalism. Democrats typically believe in a much broader role of government in the lives of people, typically focusing more on socially related issues. Libertarians believe in a government that provides minimum regulations in our day to day activities, they believe in strong civil liberties protected by government.

The health of this nation and its citizens is protected and improved by the work of the government at every level (local, state, and national). I support the position that the priority of the resources of our nation ought to be directed first toward the disadvantaged and most vulnerable. The old adage of "a chain is as strong as its weakest link" holds true in the distribution of resources of our nation. The question then should be—how do you define those who are labeled "vulnerable"? The Bible gives many clues as to what this segment of our population ought to be. The Bible clearly guides us to help the least of these. The "least of these" can be defined as given below:

Children:

But Jesus said, "Let the little children come to Me, and do not forbid them; for of such is the kingdom of heaven."

—Matthew 19:14

Behold, children are a heritage from the Lord, the fruit of the womb is a reward. Like arrows in the hand of a warrior, so are the children of one's youth.

—Psalm 127:3–4

He will bring justice to the poor of the people; He will save the children of the needy, and will break in pieces the oppressor.

—Psalm 72:4

A good man leaves an inheritance to his children's children, but the wealth of the sinner is stored up for the righteous.

—Proverbs 13:22

Children's children are the crown of old men, and the glory of children is their father.

—Proverbs 17:6

Whoever receives one of these little children in My name receives Me; and whoever receives Me, receives not Me but Him who sent Me.

—Mark 9:37

Hungry/Poor:

For He will deliver the needy when he cries, The poor also, and him who has no helper. He will spare the poor and needy, And will save the souls of the needy.

—Psalm 72:12–13

Defend the poor and fatherless; Do justice to the afflicted and needy. Deliver the poor and needy; Free them from the hand of the wicked.

—Psalm 82:3–4

I know that the LORD will maintain the cause of the afflicted, And justice for the poor.

—Psalm 140:12

He who oppresses the poor reproaches his Maker, But he who honors Him has mercy on the needy.

—Proverbs 14:31

He who has a generous eye will be blessed, For he gives of his bread to the poor.

—Proverbs 22:9

Who executes justice for the oppressed, Who gives food to the hungry. The LORD gives freedom to the prisoners.

—Psalm 146:7

He who has pity on the poor lends to the LORD, And He will pay back what he has given.

——*Proverbs 19:17*

Whoever shuts his ears to the cry of the poor, Will also cry himself and not be heard.

——*Proverbs 21:13*

Sick:

And Jesus went about all Galilee, teaching in their synagogues, preaching the gospel of the kingdom, and healing all kinds of sickness and all kinds of disease among the people.
——*Matthew 4:23*

When evening had come, they brought to Him many who were demon-possessed. And He cast out the spirits with a word, and healed all who were sick.
——*Matthew 8:16*

He Himself took our infirmities and bore our sicknesses.
——*Matthew 8:17*

And as you go, preach, saying, "The kingdom of heaven is at hand." Heal the sick, cleanse the lepers, raise the dead, cast out demons. Freely you have received, freely give.
——*Matthew 10:7–8*

And when Jesus went out He saw a great multitude; and He was moved with compassion for them, and healed their sick.
——*Matthew 14:14*

Senior Citizen/Widows:

A father of the fatherless, a defender of widows, Is God in His holy habitation.

—Psalm 68:5

"And I will come near you for judgment; I will be a swift witness against sorcerers, against adulterers, against perjurers, against those who exploit wage earners and widows and orphans, And against those who turn away an alien—Because they do not fear Me," says the Lord of hosts.

—Malachi 3:5

Woe to you, scribes and Pharisees, hypocrites! For you devour widows' houses, and for a pretense make long prayers. Therefore you will receive greater condemnation.

—Matthew 23:14

Now in those days, when the number of the disciples was multiplying, there arose a complaint against the Hebrews by the Hellenists, because their widows were neglected in the daily distribution.

—Acts 6:1

Honor widows who are really widows. But if any widow has children or grandchildren, let them first learn to show piety at home and to repay their parents; for this is good an acceptable before God. Now she who is really a widow, and left alone, trusts in God and continues in supplications and prayers night and day.

—1 Timothy 5:3–5

Pure and undefiled religion before God and the Father is this: to visit orphans and widows in their trouble, and to keep oneself unspotted from the world.

—James 1:27

The Final Word—The Least of These:

Then the King will say to those on His right hand, "Come, you blessed of My Father, inherit the kingdom prepared for you from the foundation of the world: for I was hungry and you gave Me food; I was thirsty and you gave Me drink; I was a stranger and you took Me in; I was naked and you clothed Me; I was sick and you visited Me; I was in prison and you came to Me." Then the righteous will answer Him, saying, "Lord, when did we see You hungry and feed or thirsty and give You drink? When did we see You a stranger and take You in, or naked and clothe You? Or when did we see You sick, or in prison, and come to You?" And the King will answer and say to them, "Assuredly, I say to you, inasmuch as you did it to one of the least of these My brethren, you did it to Me."

—Matthew 25:34–40

The Scriptures thus describe the "least of these," or those most vulnerable, as the children, the hungry, the poor, the sick, the elderly, and the widowed, to name the more predominant examples. These are the people that Jesus uses in his parable about the Kingdom. Jesus says in this parable that when you bless the "least of these," you are blessing God himself.

My belief system which is informed by my interpretation of Scripture is as follows: I believe that God gives us all choices in life to do good or to do evil (Joshua 24:15; Deuteronomy 30:19; 1 Kings 18:21). I believe that all humans since the creation of the world were and are all created equal (Genesis 1:26–27; Proverbs 22:2; Acts 17:26). I believe that our number one focus in life should be the next generation, our youth (Proverbs 22:6; Matthew 18:3; Psalm 127:3–5). I believe that we are to look out for the least of these, people who are less fortunate than us (Proverbs 31:8–9; Luke 4:18–19; Deuteronomy 10:17–18; Isaiah 1:17). I believe that we ought to care for and protect our senior citizens (Exodus 20:12; James 1:27). I believe that we ought to care for the sick

(Luke 4:33–35; 5:12–14; 6:17–19; 7:2–10; 7:11–16). I believe we are duty-bound to protect the earth. I believe we are called to be good stewards over all that has been given us, big or small (Genesis1:26–31; Genesis 2:8–15). These are the things that Jesus focused on while on earth! Jesus' actions and words can be observed to understand what was most important to him.

PROGRESSION OF POLICY

DEMOCRACY

◖◗

BELIEFS

Driven by:
Family Values, Faith in God, Understanding Scripture

◖◗

IDEOLOGY

◖◗

POLICY

◖◗

POLITICS

Conclusion

But be doers of the word, and not hearers only, deceiving yourselves. For if anyone is a hearer of the word and not a doer, he is like a man observing his natural face in a mirror; for he observes himself, goes away, and immediately forgets what kind of man he was. But he who looks into the perfect law of liberty and continues in it, and is not a forgetful hearer but a doer of the work, this one will be blessed in what he does.

James 1:22–25

The world of politics is populated with elected officials who fight tooth and nail for what they believe. They stand strong in support of the values they promote. They stand strong, holding the line on issues such as abortion, marriage, health care, education, military, defense, social welfare, foreign policy, and so on. Their stances on these issues generally come from (or at least should come from) a core set of values that give direction to their policies. Not talked about in great detail are the underlying factors that lead to our politics and policies.

Elected officials fight and vote for what they believe. Democrats, Republicans, Libertarians, and so on align themselves with their party of choice because of the values that they espouse. Something at the core of the candidate, elected official, and voter causes them to identify themselves based upon common beliefs or value systems. This identification tells the world that they have a certain set of principles by which they will govern and/or legislate on a day-to-day basis. We see elected officials debating passionately on TV, but we never quite hear what brought those people to the positions they hold. Unfortunately, we typically don't get a deeper insight into the mind of the elected official.

It is important to remember that your political position will rely heavily on what you hold to be true. Again, I submit that your value system is developed by what you cherish the most. I will submit that most Americans have a basic belief in God, whether it manifests in the form of Christianity (which I profess), Judaism, Islam, Hinduism, Buddhism, or any other religion or spiritual path one may adopt. As a Christian, I follow the word of God in the form of the Bible and the teachings of Jesus. This historical document, this spiritually guided document, has formed the basis of what I accept to be truth in regards to my worldview, my understanding of right & wrong, and good & evil. It has also guided my work ethic.

What I hold true and dear to my heart is my belief in God and His influence in my life. My belief in God and my understanding of the biblical teachings of God have influenced the lion's share of my actions, behaviors, and even policy decisions in my role as an elected official.

As a reminder...the direction of government is driven by politics. The direction of politics is driven by policy. Policy is driven by the ideology of a person or group. One's ideology is developed by one's established belief system. One's belief system is established in great part by what one hears and reads. From a Christian perspective this is established by the word of God, by Scripture. What people hold true is what they will live out in their lives. Thus, it is no great stretch to think that people of faith would allow their faith to speak deeply to their world of politics.

The conclusion to the matter is that our faith is an essential component of our life. What we think, what we say, and how we think is heavily connected to our faith and what we believe. It is, therefore, no great leap to say that our faith can and should influence our politics.

This book was not meant to tell you what to believe regarding your faith and your politics. However, it is intended to open your mind to understand how your faith can and should inform your politics. It's meant to push you toward looking at your faith and the Bible and using them to help develop your stance on public policy issues.

It is important to follow the progression of activities that allow you to take the great leap from faith to politics. We first begin with a general belief in God, a belief that God is the creator of all things. It is important to know that this skeleton faith is given flesh through Scripture. The Bible gives direction to the faith we believe and espouse. It gives credence to what we accept to be right and wrong. It gives direction to the purpose and call of our lives. Thus, we develop a certain belief system based upon our faith in God and through our interpretation of Scripture. As our belief system is developed, we are able to connect certain ideological principles with our belief system. Once our ideological stances have been set, we can develop various policy positions. It is our positions on a myriad of policy matters that allow us to connect with different political groups. It is a linear progression that empowers us to take the great leap from beliefs to politics. It's not an easy matter to simply jump from faith to politics. It is one that must occur in phases. Before we can move from one level in this linear progression to the next, a certain degree of understanding of the prior level must take place.

As previously stated, I said that I would not tell you what to think, nor would I disclose in great detail my personal political ideological viewpoints. It is not my place to do so. No one in a democracy has a right to tell you what you ought to think or believe.

What makes this democracy great is that it truly represents the desires and the will of the people. Part of my goal for this book was to address the sheepish tendencies of this nation's citizenry. I describe this tendency as "sheepish" because, like sheep, many Americans have simply abdicated their democratically given responsibilities and decided to follow their elected officials and parties like sheep following a shepherd. Sheep trust the shepherd so much that they simply follow the shepherd mindlessly without any thought of the direction or pace of their journey. In a representative form of government, the proper relationship between an elected official and the general public should not be like the shepherd and the sheep. We should not mindlessly follow the elected official in whatever direction he or she may go. Exactly the opposite should occur. I will submit that the elected official should observe the general direction and feelings of the people they represent and they ought to lead accordingly. This, of course, is not a black-and-white scenario. There are many shades of gray within politics. For example, when the public is generally undecided about a general direction or feelings on a matter, I believe the public should trust the person that they have placed in position of power. There are also times when an official must make a position opposite of public sentiment when the public does not have all of the information in order to have a fully informed perspective or position.

Dr. Martin Luther King, Jr. made a statement that "the ultimate measure of a man is not where he stands in moments of comfort and convenience, but where he stands at times of challenge and controversy." Having a faith-informed political stance on issues may not always be popular. Thus you have to decide for yourself if you are ready to support publicly what you believe privately.

What I have done in *My God, My Politics* is laid out the framework by which your faith can inform your politics. Hopefully, you have been empowered to define your own political positions. You are now prepared to make it difficult for any person or party to tell you what you ought to think. You have now been equipped to engage our democracy at full capacity.

Congratulations—you are on the road to realizing the intent of our democracy. You have been equipped with the ability to decide the direction of this nation, based on your own core values, based upon what you truly believe.

Now—get to work, uncover what you believe, and let the world know!

You are now officially *UN-BOUGHT* and *UN-BOSSED*! You will now be able to tell others what you believe and explain faithfully why you believe it.

Like William Ernest Henley's "Invictus"—You are now the Master of your Fate, the Captain of your Soul!

HOMEWORK:

At the end of this book I have included a homework assignment that will allow you to record your thoughts onto paper. This exercise will push you to consider and define your core set of beliefs. It will help you translate your beliefs into an ideological perspective that will help you develop your stance on various areas of public policy. Your work is not done until you finish this final task; it is well worth the effort.

HOMEWORK

✪ Write out policy issues

✪ Research each policy issue and become familiar with the points and counterpoints

✪ Scriptural Reference
- Find Scriptures that speak to the policy issue
- Interpret Scripture
- Find original intent of Scripture—Exegesis
- Overlay original intent onto present day—Exposition

✪ Overlay original intent of Scripture and connect it with the points and counterpoints of each modern day policy issue. Do this for all the areas below:
- Role of Government
- Health Care
- Criminal Justice
- Foreign Policy
- Fiscal Policy
- Education
- Military Defense
- Environment
- Social Welfare
- Social Security
- Transportation
- Tax Policy
- The Economy . . . and more

APPENDIX

Definitions

Advocacy is: the act or process of advocating or SUPPORTING a cause or proposal

Democracy is **1 a:** government by the people; *especially* : rule of the majority **b:** a government in which the supreme power is vested in the people and exercised by them directly or indirectly through a system of representation usually involving periodically held free elections

Belief is **1:** a state or habit of mind in which trust or confidence is placed in some person or thing **2:** something believed; *especially*: a tenet or body of tenets held by a group **3:** conviction of the truth of some statement or the reality of some being or phenomenon especially when based on examination of evidence

Exposition is **1:** a setting forth of the meaning or purpose (as of a writing) **2:** discourse or an example of it designed to convey information or explain what is difficult to understand

Government is **a:** the organization, machinery, or agency through which a political unit exercises authority and performs functions and which is usually classified according to the distribution of power within it **b:** the complex of political institutions, laws, and customs through which the function of governing is carried out.

Governing is **1a:** to exercise continuous sovereign authority over; especially: to control and direct the making and administration of policy in **b:** to rule without sovereign power and unusually without having the authority to determine basic policy

Hermeneutic is **1**: the STUDY of the methodological principles of interpretation (as of the Bible) **2:** A method or principle of interpretation

Ideology is **1**: visionary theorizing **2a**: a systematic body of concepts especially about human life or culture **b**: a manner or the content of thinking characteristic of an individual, group, or culture **c**: the integrated assertions, theories and aims that constitute a sociopolitical program

Justice is **1a:** the maintenance or administration of what is just especially by the impartial adjustment of conflicting CLAIMS or the assignment of merited rewards or punishments **b:** JUDGE *c* **:** the administration of law; *especially* **:** the establishment or determination of rights according to the rules of law or equity **2a:** the QUALITY of being just, impartial, or fair **b(1)** **:** the principle or ideal of just dealing or right action **b(2)** **:** conformity to this principle or ideal **:** RIGHTEOUSNESS *c* **:** the quality of conforming to law **3:** conformity to truth, fact, or reason **:** CORRECTNESS

Law is **1a**: a binding custom or practice of a community: a rule of conduct or action prescribed or formally recognized as binding or enforced by a controlling authority **b**: the whole body of such customs, practices, or rules

Politics is the art or science of government; it is the art or science concerned with guiding or influencing governmental policy; and it is also the art or science concerned with winning and holding control over a government.

Policy is **1a**: prudence or wisdom in the management of affairs **b**: management or procedure based primarily on material interest **2a**: a definite course or method of action selected from among alternatives and in light of given conditions to guide and determine present and future decisions **b**: a high-level overall plan embracing the general goals and acceptable procedures especially of a governmental body

Social Policy is the guidelines and interventions for the changing, maintenance or creation of living conditions that are conducive to human welfare. Thus, social policy is that part of public policy that has to do with social issues.

Theocracy is **1**: government of a state by immediate divine guidance or by officials who are regarded as divinely guided **2**: a state governed by a theocracy

ABOUT THE AUTHOR

Lee May is both an elected official and a minister of the Gospel. He was elected in 2006 and currently serves as the Deputy Presiding Officer for the DeKalb County Commission. He has a Masters of Divinity degree from Emory University's Candler School of Theology and a B.A. in Business Administration from Clark Atlanta University.

As Commissioner, Lee May and his colleagues oversee a billion-dollar budget, and he represents over 160,000 residents located in the heart of one of the most affluent African-American communities in the country. As a leader in ministry, Lee May serves as one of the youngest ordained Elders at his local church.

Lee May is married to his wife, Robin, and is father to daughters Ryann Kimberly and Reagan Leanne.

For more information about the author, Lee May you can follow him as follows:

Website:www.MyGodMyPolitics.com
Twitter:www.twitter.com/MyGodMyPolitics
Facebook:www.facebook.com/MyGodMyPolitics

To book Lee May as a speaker email: book@mygodmypolitics.com

CPSIA information can be obtained at www.ICGtesting.com
Printed in the USA
239085LV00001B/3/P